Volume I

THE
UNIVERSAL CHURCH
IN
GOD'S DESIGN

MAN'S DISORDER AND GOD'S DESIGN

The Amsterdam Assembly Series

I. THE UNIVERSAL CHURCH IN GOD'S DESIGN

i. The Doctrine of the Church. ii. Shame and Glory. iii. Signs of His Appearing. iv. The Ecumenical Movement.

by G. AULÉN, KARL BARTH, C. T. CRAIG, P. DEVANANDAN, A. FJELLBU, G. FLOROVSKY, J. GREGG, RICHARD NIEBUHR, E. SCHLINK, K. E. SKYDS-GAARD, W. A. VISSER 'T HOOFT, OLIVER TOMKINS, M. VILLAIN, OLIVE WYON.

II. THE CHURCH'S WITNESS TO GOD'S DESIGN

i. The Church's Commission. ii. Our un-Christian World. iii. Some Axioms of the Modern Man. iv. The Relevance of the Gospel. v. The Gospel at Work. vi. The Approach to Other Faiths.

by FRANK BENNETT, EMIL BRUNNER, W. M. HORTON, H. KRAEMER, PIERRE MAURY, S. C. NEILL, L. NEWBIGIN, W. PAUCK, S. SAVARIMUTHU, P. TILLICH, G. VICEDOM.

III. THE CHURCH AND THE DISORDER OF SOCIETY

i. God's Design and the Present Disorder. ii. Technics and Civilization. iii. The Situation in Europe, Asia and U.S.A. iv. Personal Relations in a Technical Society. v. The Involvement of the Church. vi. New Beginnings in the relations of the Church to Society. vii. A Responsible Society. viii. The Strategy of the Church.

by S. BATES, J. C. BENNETT, KATHLEEN BLISS, EMIL BRUNNER, J. ELLUL, REINHOLD NIEBUHR, J. H. OLDHAM, C. L. PATIJN, M. M. THOMAS, E. C. URWIN.

IV. THE CHURCH AND THE INTERNATIONAL DISORDER

i. The Churches' Approach to International Affairs. ii. The Disorder of International Society. iii. Christian Responsibility in our Divided World. iv. Freedom of Religion and Related Human Rights. v. Christian Responsibility in a World of Power.

by R. P. BARNES, E. BRUNNER, JOHN FOSTER DULLES, K. G. GRUBB, J. L. HROMADKA, O. F. NOLDE, F. M. VAN ASBECK.

V. THE OFFICIAL ASSEMBLY REPORT

THE
UNIVERSAL CHURCH
IN
GOD'S DESIGN

AN

ECUMENICAL STUDY

PREPARED UNDER THE AUSPICES OF THE

WORLD COUNCIL OF CHURCHES

HARPER & BROTHERS
PUBLISHERS · NEW YORK

First published 1948

Distributed in Canada by
The Macmillan Company of Canada Limited
70 Bond Street, Toronto

Printed in Great Britain by
Northumberland Press Limited
Gateshead on Tyne

GENERAL PREFACE

THIS book, with its companion volumes, was written in preparation for the First Assembly of the World Council of Churches in Amsterdam, Holland, August 22—September 4, 1948.

Two years and a half in advance of the Assembly, the Provisional Committee of the Council determined that the main theme for the Assembly should be:

MAN'S DISORDER AND GOD'S DESIGN

and that this theme should be considered under four aspects:

1. The Universal Church in God's Design.
2. The Church's Witness to God's Design.
3. The Church and the Disorder of Society.
4. The Church and the International Disorder.

These topics were not chosen at random. They represent burning concerns of all the churches in this crisis of civilization. The first reveals the growing determination of the various churches to rediscover the divine intention for the Church, and the right relationship of the various churches to one another. Of that determination, the World Council itself is both an evidence and a concrete result. The second testifies to the obligation recognized by all churches alike to claim for Christ the whole world and all aspects of life. From the outset it has been recognized that the World Council would be still-born unless evangelism were its life-blood. The third and fourth subjects bring Christian faith directly to bear upon two critical areas of disorder in contemporary civilization, the social and the international. They deal with the familiar query: What has the Church to contribute to society in its present extremity?

Preparation of the delegates for the consideration of these issues at Amsterdam was entrusted to the Study Department Commission of the World Council of Churches. Commissions consisting of leading Christians, both clerical and lay, from various parts of the world, were formed to deal with the four topics. Each Commission held two meetings and came together

again on the eve of the Assembly for the final stages of preparation. A volume was outlined on each topic, and writers of
chapters were carefully selected. In almost every instance, their
contributions have been subjected to searching criticism by the
Commission concerned, both individually and corporately, and
by a considerably wider circle of experts. In most cases, chapters
have been rewritten in the light of this truly ecumenical scrutiny
at least once, in some instances two or more times. Thus, the
volumes which are here presented represent the outcome of a
comprehensive interchange of thought and conviction among
leaders of virtually all Christian Communions (except the
Roman Catholic). It will be understood that in these circumstances the World Council of Churches itself is not committed
to the opinions expressed in the volumes.

But quite apart from its literary results, the process of
ecumenical thinking possesses in itself an educational and in-
spirational value which should not be underestimated. Especially
for people in isolated areas of the world, this interchange of
documents and comments means an opportunity, eagerly
grasped, to share in a vital conversation with brethren from
other churches and countries. The wide interest taken in the
theme of the Assembly is also evidenced by the fact that several
collaborating groups are now preparing similar volumes, dealing
with the same set of subjects from a national or confessional
perspective.

All these studies are founded on earlier work—the sequence
of ecumenical conferences of the past two decades, especially the
Oxford Conference on " Church, Community and State " in
1937, the patient enquiries of the Faith and Order movement,
the labour of ecumenical study groups in many lands, and the
programme of the Study Department of the World Council
which continued, hampered but unabated, through all the years
of the war.

Serious effort has been made to assure that this discussion
be truly ecumenical, representative equally of Christian churches
in every part of the world. But difficulties of effective communication have to a considerable degree frustrated that aim.
It has not been possible to secure as many contributions as was
hoped from the Eastern Orthodox world and from the churches
of Asia, Africa and Latin America. This limitation, while real
and regrettable, is less grave than might at first be supposed.

For no fact stands out more clearly than that, in the basic problems confronted both by the churches and by the societies in which they are set, ours is in truth one world.

Although the volumes of the present series were prepared to serve the particular occasion of the Amsterdam Assembly, they deal with issues of continuing and urgent importance for the whole of Christendom. It is hoped, therefore, that they may have a wide usefulness beyond and after the Assembly, and they are here presented to all thoughtful people, within and outside the churches, for that purpose.

GENERAL INTRODUCTION

THE World Council of Churches has come into being at a moment of peril for all mankind which is without precedent in the whole of human history. Frustration and fear grip the minds of men and women. This is true not only of the masses who feel themselves caught in a fate over which they have no power, but hardly less of their leaders who hold in their hands the guidance of events which they are unable to control.

At this fateful moment, the theme of the first Assembly of the Council—MAN'S DISORDER AND GOD'S DESIGN—is singularly relevant and needs little interpretation.

MAN'S DISORDER is inescapably manifest in every aspect of the world's life to-day. It is not merely a result of the recent war. Before the war, the sickness of civilization was far advanced. The disappearance of common standards, the denial of a law of God above the wills of men and states, the disintegration of family life, the dissolution of community, loss of faith save the false faith in human wisdom and goodness, emptiness and meaninglessness in the souls of men—these symptoms of sickness were clear enough. At almost every point, war and its aftermath have aggravated MAN'S DISORDER. And now has been added the greatest dread of all, that man's mastery of atomic energy foreshadows the annihilation of man and all his works.

The Church carries a large share of responsibility for MAN'S DISORDER; and it is for that responsibility that the churches must give account. This is true: if the churches had been faithful to their commission from Christ, if they had spoken the word of truth committed to them, if they had rightly interpreted to the world the causes of its sickness, if they had ministered to the world grace and power, above all if they had manifested in their own life the only true medicine for the healing of the nations— if they had done all this, humanity might not have come to its present extremity. On the contrary, MAN'S DISORDER finds its most pointed expression in the disorder of the Church itself.

We live in an age when the Christian Church in many parts is rediscovering its divine mission. But precisely at that moment it discovers its own weaknesses. To men whose deepest need is spiritual rebirth, it has not exhibited the power of the Spirit.

To a world whose deepest need is community, the Church which claims to be the Body of Christ, professing one Lord, one faith, one baptism, one God and Father of all, has presented division and disunity. These are sins for which the Church is responsible to God and to man. Its first act must therefore be, not condemnation of the world, but confession and contrition.

In this plight, our only hope lies in GOD'S DESIGN, His design for the world and for the Church.

GOD'S DESIGN is the divine purpose for men and nations, manifest in the acts of God in Christ. In His life, death and resurrection, in the coming of the Church and the outpouring of the Holy Spirit, a new beginning has been made in human history. In Him, God has begun a work of new creation and redemption. In Him, a reign of love and forgiveness has been inaugurated, moulding the hearts and lives of men, calling them to find their common centre and desire in Him, and so to discover that real community for which mankind is longing. In Him, the Church is continuously reborn from death to life. In Him, there is also revealed GOD'S DESIGN for the ordering of human society, a design that is an act both of judgment and of redemption.

Adopting MAN'S DISORDER AND GOD'S DESIGN as the theme for its first Assembly and as the title of the present series of volumes, the World Council of Churches has committed itself to a double task. It must seek to comprehend MAN'S DISORDER in the light of GOD'S DESIGN, in order that the churches may mediate to the world both a true understanding of its distress and the grace and power to find a way out. And it must bring the churches to face, with relentless realism, their involvement in the world's folly as well as their own distinctive disorders, in order that they may be ready to receive from God the rebirth and true unity which He purposes for them.

HENRY P. VAN DUSEN
President of Union Theological Seminary
Chairman of the Study Department Commission

CONTENTS

CONTRIBUTORS

AULÉN, Gustaf, D.D., Bishop of Strängnäs, Sweden; formerly Professor of Systematic Theology at University of Lund. Author of *Christus Victor*, etc.

BARTH, Karl, D.THEOL., Professor of Theology at the University of Basel. Author of *Kirchliche Dogmatik*, etc.

CRAIG, Clarence, D.D., Professor of New Testament, Yale University. Author of *The Study of the New Testament*, etc.

DEVANANDAN, Paul D., PH.D., Professor of History of Religions at the United Theological College, Bangalore. Author of *The Concept of Maya*, etc.

FJELLBU, Arne, D.D., Bishop of Nidaros, Trondheim, Norway; formerly secretary of Norwegian Student Christian Movement. Author of *Sielesorg, Den kristne Moral*, etc.

FLOROVSKY, George, D.D., Professor of Dogmatics, Orthodox Theological Institute, Paris. Author of *Eastern Fathers of the Fourth Century* (Russian), and *The Ways of Russian Theology* (French), etc.

GREGG, J. A. F., D.D., Archbishop of Armagh and Primate of all Ireland; formerly Professor of Divinity at Trinity College, Dublin. Author of *Decian Persecution, The Wisdom of Solomon*, etc.

NIEBUHR, H. Richard, PH.D., Professor of Christian Ethics, Yale University. Author of *The Social Sources of Denominationalism, The Meaning of Revelation*, etc.

SCHLINK, Edmund, D.THEOL., Professor of Systematic Theology and Director of Ecumenical Institute at the University of Heidelberg. Author of *Bekennende Kirche und Welt*, etc.

SKYDSGAARD, Kristen E., D.D., Professor at University of Copenhagen. Author of *Metafysik og Tro; en dogmatisk Studie i nyere Thomisme*.

TOMKINS, Oliver S., Assistant General Secretary of World Council of Churches; formerly Editor of *Student Movement* Magazine.

VILLAIN, Maurice, DR. EN THÉOL.

VISSER 'T HOOFT, W. A., D.D., General Secretary of World Council of Churches. Author of *The Kingship of Christ*, etc.

WYON, Olive, D.D., Secretary of Study Department of World Council of Churches. Author of *The School of Prayer*, etc.

INTRODUCTION

THE CHURCH IN THE WORLD TO-DAY

I N the hopeless world of our time, the one hope lies in the Church of Christ. This appears to be a fantastic claim. Nevertheless, we make it. It is for this reason that an Assembly of Churches, meeting on a world-wide scale in the year 1948, puts the question of the Church itself in the forefront of its consideration. For us, who meet, this is inevitable. We meet because we believe that the Church of Jesus Christ is the greatest reality on earth, and we belong to it.

It is the ground and justification of our coming together. From many countries and cultures, in spite of deep differences and even disagreements, the language we possess is the language of the Church; it is the language of the Bible, of prayer, of our fathers in the faith. For us the Church is certainly no mere idea. It is a strong reality of history and of geography. From whatever tradition we come, our roots lie deep in the past; recent years have seen the Church in many countries emerge from suffering and persecution with a deepened awareness of its own essential nature; recent centuries have seen the spread and growth of the Christian churches in lands where, a few generations ago, they were unknown; more recently, churches which often seemed strange, foreign growths have become a true part of the native life of the cultures which they invaded. Above all, and in all this, the Church is first and last the point in our experience at which eternity penetrates time, and where history gains meaning, for it is the point at which the Living God has condescended to continue meeting us; it is the point at which the Word Who once became Flesh is still to be encountered.

We know well that to many minds among our contemporaries, this preoccupation of Christians with the Church must appear to be not only unwarrantably self-centred, but even completely irrelevant. Such minds, assessing the great forces that are stirring in the world of 1948, do not consider the Christian Church as a relevant factor. To some, in so far as it is relevant, it is mischievous, because it represents the last stronghold of many ideas that are rightly doomed. A few pay it the compliment of considering it dangerous. Far more feel they can safely ignore it in any estimate of the resources of men to face mankind's own problem in our time.

Such men can call much witness to their support. The Christian churches have emerged with an ambiguous record in the development of science in recent centuries; now opposing it blindly; now capitulating without reserve to its findings; at all times speaking with an uncertain voice. In the great political and economic conflict of our time, Christian witness is again divided. Confronted with Communism, Christian bodies speak with contradictory voices or maintain a discreet silence. In the tidal-wave of nascent nationalism in the rising powers of Africa and the East, the Church appears again either to be inextricably confused with the western, alien domination which is being repudiated, or else to be a negligible force in the nationalisms which engulf it. In every major crisis of our time, the Church may thus appear as irrelevant and impotent. Can a World Assembly of Christians justify putting *the Church* in the fore-front of the picture? Indeed, is an Assembly of Churches of any importance to the world of 1948? These are questions which many minds will expect to have answered, and Christians cannot deny that they are questions which have a right to be asked.

It is true to say that the Christian Church makes high claims for itself. It is truer to say that the Gospel makes high claims for the Church; and the Church cannot ignore any claim made by the Gospel, even when it is a claim relating to itself. The Gospel claims that God, Who has made and still rules the world, has won a victory in history itself against the forces which oppose Him. This took place when God raised from death a certain Jesus of Nazareth, vindicating Him as His "anointed one" and gave Him universal Lordship. Although men may deny it, Jesus Christ *is* Lord and human history is the scene of His Lordship. Human history is also the story of Christ's waiting. His sovereignty is yet to be shown in unmistakable power. Meanwhile He has given to a community, which lives in history, the duty to proclaim His rule and the power to exhibit it to all who can grasp the real meaning of what God has done through Him. God acts in history and the Church holds the thread running through it which gives a clue to its meaning.

In various times and at various places, the hidden meaning

becomes clearer. There are times when human society becomes so corrupt and so lawless, when institutions of justice and humanity so break down, that the Church's clue which leads to the Author of order and love is more readily seen. There are times when man's inability to transcend his own limitations makes clearer the dependence of Christians upon a power and a capacity for renewal which come from beyond themselves. There are times when the bitter conflicts which divide men are more nearly transcended and more quickly healed within the Christian community than outside it.

We claim that our own time has been one of such times. Although we admit, with as much honesty and insight as have been given us, the extent to which the disorders of the world have infected the Christian community, we are still able to claim that God has shown amongst us powers of resistance, healing and unification for which we claim no credit for ourselves but give glory to Him.

The story of the "Christian resistance" in many countries during recent years can be read in two versions. To some it will appear only that organized Christianity showed unexpected resilience and boldness, not only in resisting Nazi invaders of other countries, but even in resisting the rise and spread of Marxism in Germany itself. Professor Einstein, from outside the Christian ranks, paid an ungrudging tribute to the way in which the churches stood and fought when political parties, trades unions and universities had capitulated. He spoke in terms which many have been ready to endorse. But we also claim that the "Christian resistance" has a deeper meaning. It is the meaning of Christian *renewal*. For those who accept the Lordship of Jesus Christ over all human life, the struggle is of wider significance than the war itself; it is the dramatic sharpening of a struggle that is always going on between the Kingdom of Christ and all man-centred systems. For this reason, the struggle is not over. The temptations to relax, to subside into controversy over lesser issues, to lose the unity of the days of conflict, to look back to easier times instead of moving forward into uncertain ones, these are to be expected, but they are to be resisted and overcome if the struggle is seen in its full Christian dimensions. Christian renewal is not a past event to look back on: it is a quality of life in which always to live.

War proved powerless to break the unity in which Christians

are bound together. Although there were some who completely subordinated their universal loyalty to Christ to the claim of nationalism, there remained strong expressions of the transcending unity. Churches supported the missionary work of enemy nationals; prisoners of war received, in the name of Christ, spiritual ministrations from their enemies; even before the war had ended, ecumenical plans were made for reconstruction and inter-church aid; within a few months of the cessation of fighting, both in Europe and Asia, the work of reconciliation had begun; Christians were meeting again, face to face, to resume interrupted conversation on their uninterrupted common tasks. We believe that these facts, and many more, point to a deep unity to which we must give ever clearer expression.

And so, above all, we believe that the Spirit which has been at work amongst Christians for some decades, leading them into continually closer co-operation and understanding, has found clearest symbolic expression in the World Council of Churches. We believe that this council is but one aspect of a wider and deeper activity of the same Spirit of God in our time, working far beyond the limits of our formally organized fellowship and in ways which we have yet to recognize.

We claim that God is working amongst His chosen community for their *renewal* and their *unity* in ways some of which we can already discern. Because He is the Lord of Creation, as well as Lord of the Church, we claim that what is happening to us is also of unpredictable significance for the whole of mankind.

We belong to the Church: the Church does not belong to us. We claim that the hope of the world lies in the Church because the only hope of man lies in the love of God and the Church is that area of human life where man responds to God's love. In spite of all its failure, cowardice, and even betrayal, the Church remains the place in human life where man admits that he does not belong to himself. The fear and pain of the world, in 1948 or in any other year, meet their answer only in that community which truly understands that we belong to Christ and Christ belongs to God, Whose love is our hope.

I

THE DOCTRINE OF THE CHURCH:
SOME INTERPRETATIONS

———

The fundamental problem of the Church is the existence of the churches. This is not an abstract, theological proposition; it is our admission of a fact of life.

The first fact to face is that there is no agreed Christian interpretation of the doctrine of the Church. Even the Church which has the strongest appearance of unity and the most exclusive claims in the face of other Christians, the Church of Rome, has no dogmatic definition of its theology of the Church.

In this section we lay bare the dilemma from which we start. Five scholars have here interpreted, briefly, the biblical evidence for the nature of the Church. None of them writes as an official spokesman of his tradition; none claims any other authority than his personal authority as a theologian, standing in a particular tradition. They differ in important respects in their conclusions. But they illustrate the situation in Christendom to-day.

But, as it would be untrue to conceal their differences, it would be equally untrue to minimize their agreements. The whole history of the ecumenical movement testifies to the wide area of Christian agreement and to its continual enlargement and definition.

These essays must be read in the context of the whole work of the Faith and Order movement, especially the Declaration of Unity of the Edinburgh Conference 1937. It is only the unity which exists that makes possible the exploration of our differences. It is only the unity which we believe that God has already given which affords hope that the honest search for biblical truth will, not create unity, but more and more reveal it.

1

THE CHURCH IN THE LIGHT OF THE NEW TESTAMENT

by Gustaf Aulén

I JESUS AND THE CHURCH

IN the New Testament, Christianity appears in the form of the Church. To be a Christian is to be a member of the Church, to have a share in the new *koinonia*, the new communion. However, the question has been raised about the relationship between this Church and Jesus Himself. Sometimes exegesis has denied the existence of such a relationship. It has been said that Jesus had no intention of creating a Church, and that the idea of a Church was quite unfamiliar to His teaching and to His aims. An interpretation of the Gospels that does not recognize any connection between Jesus and the Church cannot be maintained. Such an interpretation misunderstands the central message of the Gospel.

Jesus appears as the Messiah of Israel. His task was to fulfil God's promises to His people. He did not come to teach a new religious doctrine, but to proclaim a *message* and deliver an invitation: " The time is fulfilled, and the Kingdom of God is at hand: repent ye and believe the Gospel " (Mark i, 15). He addressed His invitation to His people, to Israel. When He called individuals, He called them to be disciples, to enter the messianic people that He gathered around Himself, to enter the new *koinonia*, the chosen people, the true Israel, that would share in the fulfilment of the promises.

As regards Jesus and the Church, we must not confine our investigations to the statements which speak directly about the *ecclesia*. It is much more important to observe how the idea of a new fellowship continually appears in the Gospels, and how it represents there a constitutive element. Some few examples may be mentioned: Jesus speaks of Himself as the bridegroom among the wedding guests, He speaks of the wedding feast, of the temple to be built (Mark xiv, 58), of the corner-stone that has been laid. Other examples are actions such as the calling of the

Twelve, the sending out of the apostles as authorized agents, the feeding of the five thousand, the Last Supper and so on. The idea of the Church, the *koinonia*, gathered around the Messiah, is indissolubly united with the idea of the Messiah. In the Gospels we find everywhere the consciousness of a new, super-individual order, a new continuity, created by and based upon Christ. This continuity cannot be considered as only an idea, as an invisible continuity. On the contrary, it was something very concrete and realistic: Jesus Himself with His apostles and dis-ciples. In and through this *koinonia* the individual was made a participant in the new age (*aeon*), the Kingdom of God, the new life and the glory to come. The Church that appeared through the events of Pentecost had not only relation to certain statements and actions of Jesus, but was inseparably connected with His appearance as Messiah, as Christ. The continuity between Jesus and the apostolic Church is unbroken. This statement can be denied, but only if we deny that Jesus appeared as Messiah. No Messiah can exist without an *ecclesia* belonging to him. Therefore, faith in Christ and the *koinonia* of the Church belong necessarily together. The realm belongs to the King.

II THE CHURCH AS THE BODY OF CHRIST

The biblical view of the Church is most comprehensively ex-pressed in the formula: the Body of Christ, *soma Christou*. When the Church is called the Body of Christ, that means first of all that Christ and the Church belong together as an insepar-able unity. The Church has its existence in and through Christ, and just as we cannot imagine the Church without Christ, so we cannot imagine Christ-Kyrios without His domination, without the communion that belongs to Him. Where Christ is, there is also His Church: and where the Church is, there Christ is found also. Communion with Christ is a communion in and through the Church. Christ is incarnate in His Church. The Church, while subject to the conditions of this earth and this time, is the revelation of the living and active Christ. Here He meets us and works with us.

Therefore, when the Church is called the Body of Christ, this expression is not to be understood merely as figurative. This word visualizes in a very concrete way that Christ and the Church are a unity. It tells us that Christ is living in the Church and

at the same time gives life to the Church. When Christ in the
Epistles to the Ephesians and Colossians is described as "the
Head"—"He is the head of the body, His church" (Col. i, 18)
—the intention is not to describe how Christ is separated from
the Church, to separate the head and the body as two different
parts. On the contrary, the intention is to emphasize their in-
separable continuity and unity. Christ is not the isolated head,
but the head of His body. And the Church is not the body as
isolated from the head, but the Body of Christ. The Body of
Christ is Christ Himself, the Risen Christ, alive and active on
earth. As the Head of the Body He is the authority that every
member has to serve and to obey. He is the life-giving power
and the living hope of the Church.

We find the same view of the relation between Christ and the
Church in many other biblical expressions, for instance in the
words of St. John about the vine and the branches, and in the
words in the Epistle to the Ephesians about the Church as a holy
temple in the Lord: "Christ himself being the chief corner
stone: in whom all the building fitly framed together groweth
into a holy temple in the Lord" (Eph. ii, 20-21).

All these three statements about the Church emphasize not
only the unity of the Church and Christ, but also the communion
of Christians within the Church. The body has many different
members with different tasks, but they are all part of the same
body. All the branches belong to the same vine, and thus have
communion with each other. The stones do not lie isolated. As
"living stones" they are joined together in a holy temple, each
fitted into its place. Therefore these symbols also represent the
communion of the members in the Church. But this communion depends wholly and entirely upon communion with
Christ.

III THE CHURCH AND THE NEW AGE

The *koinonia* of the Church means that a new age has
appeared in this world of sin and death. God has given mankind
a new beginning when He gave us Christ as Lord and made Him
the Head of a new humanity. To be a member of the Church
means to have been made a participant, in this new age, of the
regnum Christi that at the same time is a *regnum gratiae*. It
means to have received the gift of the justification that Christ

has acquired through His sacrifice and His victory over the devil and all the evil forces in the world. Opposing the dominion of sin and death and the old Age, stands the dominion of grace and life, ruling by "the righteousness of God" (Rom. i, 17).

However, the old Age has not disappeared. It is still existing here on earth. But in the midst of this old Age the Church as *regnum Christi* represents the new Age. The Church is not *of* the world, but she lives *in* the world. Because "grace and truth came through Jesus Christ" (John i, 17), she lives in the age of fulfilment. Because she still lives in the old Age of sin and death, she lives in a permanent fight against the evil forces of destruction, and the fulfilment that has come is at the same time a promise of a glory to come when the Kingdom of God will be wholly and entirely realized. Therefore the view of the Church, living and fighting in this world, is an eschatological view. The Church exists on the border between two worlds, having part in the misery of this world, and at the same time having a quality that transcends every present age of history.

As members of the Church, Christians live in two worlds. Living in the "old Age", in "Adam", the Christian is a sinner, mixed up in the sinfulness of the world. Living in the new Age, *in regnum gratiae*, he is redeemed and justified, transferred from the kingdom of darkness to the Kingdom of the Son of God's love. As long as the Christian lives here in this world he must, therefore, wage a permanent struggle against sin and the whole nature of the world, the power of which, however, is broken through Christ.

This duality will last until the new Age is fulfilled in glory. The Christian is, according to the view of the New Testament, *simul justus et peccator*, at the same time justified and a sinner. This formula from the Reformation is quite in harmony with the realistic view of the New Testament. The New Testament speaks very openly about the sins, divisions and infirmities to be found in the Church. At the same time it speaks of the Church as one in Christ, as holy and as a communion of saints. The Church is a "Communion of Saints", not in the sense that her members are holy or "saintly" from a moralistic point of view, not in the sense that they are "perfect"; but the Church is called the Communion of Saints because Christ as the head of the Church is her holiness, and because His Holy Spirit is active in the Church for the sanctification of her members.

IV THE CONSTITUTIVE ELEMENTS OF THE CHURCH

The New Testament gives us a very clear view of the constitutive elements of the Church. The Church that was revealed as a living reality on the first Whit-Sunday was a creation of the Holy Spirit, working through the divine message concerning the victorious Christ as Saviour and Lord. This message appeared in double shape, as Word and as Sacrament, holy action. The gift of the Spirit was the sign that the new Age had come, and that the promises to the Fathers had been fulfilled. The Church was constituted as a community of the baptized, gathered around the Holy Communion as the centre of their worship.

The Church was born into life as a spiritual continuity where the forces of the divine forgiveness and the world to come were at work. In the same way the message about Christ was spread around the world by the apostles and their assistants and successors. And everywhere the Sacraments appeared as an essential part of the life of the Church. Therefore, according to the New Testament, the constitutive factors of the Church are the Word of God and the Sacraments of Baptism and the Eucharist. The Word and the Sacraments are bearers of the divine action. The Spirit, working through Word and Sacraments, uses the apostles and their assistants and successors as instruments and servants. The Word and the Sacraments claim the ministry as their servant.

V THE WORD OF GOD

Primarily the Word of God is Christ Himself. He is, as the only-begotten, the Word in a unique sense, from the beginning being with the Father. When Christ appeared on earth, the Word of God was incarnate. "The Word became flesh and dwelt among us, full of grace and truth" (John i, 14). This incarnate Word is the foundation of the Church—"For other foundation can no man lay than that is laid, which is Jesus Christ" (1 Cor. iii, 11).

However, this same Word speaks to us and acts with us in the message given to us in the Bible, in the *Gospel*. Therefore, also this message appears as the Word of God and as the basis and life-giving power of the Church for all ages and generations.

Everything in the message proclaimed by the apostles has its centre in Christ. That is true also when the message of the apostles refers to the Old Testament scriptures. The Old Testament then appears as a witness to Christ as "the One who is to come". It is interpreted in the light of God's act fulfilled in Christ, to which the apostolic message bears testimony.

The meaning of the Word of God as Gospel would be completely misunderstood if considered only as a doctrine. The Gospel appears as the witness of the apostles and as the message about Christ delivered by them as "ambassadors on behalf of Christ". In the New Testament we find this message in all its purity and firmness. But at the same time it is not only a human message. Christ Himself is in the Gospel. He is Himself the Gospel and through the Gospel He follows up His work among and with us. Therefore the words of the message are "living words", "the words of eternal life" (John vi, 68). When Christ is at work in and through the Gospel, God releases man from the bonds of darkness and leads him through the faith that He kindles into the *Regnum gratiae* whose Lord and Head is Christ, where peace and joy and hope reign.

According to this biblical view, the Christian conception of the Word must reject theories that mechanize the Word, and fail to see that the Word appears in the form of a human witness, as well as theories according to which the character of the divine message appears in a spiritualized way. The Spirit speaks in and through the Word. Only in this way is the Spirit given. The Spirit speaks and acts in and through the Word. A Spirit outside the Word and independent of the Word of God is not God's holy Spirit.

The Word of God does not appear only as Gospel. It appears also as Law. They both pertain to the Church, but in different ways. The Law of God is the Law of creation, *of the Creator*. It would lead to misunderstandings if we were to describe this Law as a "natural" Law. But certainly it is a universal Law. It expresses the claim of God on mankind: the claim of Love, that at the same time is the foundation of justice. It is manifested not only in "commandments", but also in the wrath of God, "that is revealed from heaven against all ungodliness and wickedness of men who by their wickedness suppress the truth" (Rom. i, 18).

The Law has been in force since "the beginning". The Gospel on the other hand has its foundation in the promises of God. Because of these promises the Church existed in a pre-

paratory way even under the Old Covenant. But until the
fulness of the Gospel appeared in Christ, the Church did not
appear as a living reality. The Gospel is building the Church
on earth. The Gospel gives the Church her life. Through the
Gospel the Church is what she is. However, that does not mean
that the Law should have no place in the Church, or that it
should be only a matter of secondary importance.

Certainly, from one point of view the Law has been abolished.
When St. Paul says that Christ is the end of the Law, that means
that the Law is no way to salvation, and that the Law has no
right to condemn the man who has been justified by faith in
Christ. The Law is abolished *in loco justificationis*, but only
there. Otherwise the Law remains in all its power and in all
its universal importance. Through the Law, God has declared
His will as regards our human relationships. It may here
especially be emphasized that the Law of God functions also
outside the Church as a *dynamis* for promoting justice and crush-
ing injustice. However, it is the responsibility of the Church as
regards all human relationships to keep watch over the sanctity
of the Law of God. It is also the duty of the Church, in the ever-
changing situations, to interpret the divine Law according to the
revelation of God given to the Church.

VI BAPTISM

In the Sacraments, the divine Love gives itself to us through
an action.

Through the Sacraments Christ incorporates us with Himself
as members of His Body, the Church.

Fundamental and elemental incorporation in the Body of
Christ takes place through baptism. By nature we are members
of sinful humanity and subject to its conditions. Through
baptism we are brought into a wholly new relation. We become
members of the Body of Christ according to the words of St.
Paul: "for by one Spirit we were all baptized into one Body"
(1 Cor. xii, 13). Thus we are born into a new existence given to
us through Christ.

However, baptism is not only an act of initiation. It embraces
the Christian life in its entirety. It means that the Christian
life must be a continually repeated dying with Christ and rising
with Him. The baptized can remain a living member in Christ

only in this way, as a living branch of the true vine (Rom. vi, 5-11).   As long as the baptized lives on earth, he has to live his life infected by sin and unbelief.   The Covenant of Baptism is still in force as far as God is concerned, and it is continually calling man through repentance to return to the grace of God as manifested already in baptism.

As the act of incorporation, baptism is an action of the divine *gratia preveniens*: the call of God is the foundation of our membership.   It is from this point of view that we must consider the baptism of infants.   For the baptism of infants shows us how our membership in the Church has its basis not in our own endeavours and efforts, but solely in the divine Love and grace, and therefore also how this membership is quite independent of human judgments and decisions.   At the same time this kind of baptism acts, and must act, as a living conscience in the Church, impressing upon her her duty to take care of the baptized and to give them a Christian education.

As regards the question of the baptism of infants in the Early Church, it seems very probable that such was sometimes the practice already in the time of the New Testament.   It is said more than once that someone was baptized with all his family, that is, with wife and children.   When the Gospel tells us that Jesus rebuked His disciples because they would hinder the children from coming to Him, it does not seem unlikely that this statement has been preserved because the Early Church here found a justification of the baptism of infants.   However, for the justification of infant baptism it is not necessary to refer to isolated statements in the New Testament.   The justification has its foundation in the Gospel itself as the Gospel of the free and undeserved grace of God.   This Gospel and the baptism of infants belong together.[1]

VII   THE EUCHARIST

As an introduction it ought to be emphasized that the institution of the Eucharist on the night when the Lord was betrayed must not be considered as an isolated action.   It must be seen

[1] It must be remarked, at this point, that critics of this paper who belong to the Baptist tradition, consider these interpretations of the New Testament evidence or of the doctrine of grace to be untenable.   For the Baptist interpretation see *The Ministry and Sacraments*, pp. 219-229 (Student Christian Movement Press, 1937).

in connection with earlier holy table communion between Jesus, His disciples and others.

In the Gospel of St. Mark we find that Jesus in the Last Supper would assure His disciples of the continued personal communion between Himself and His disciples. As regards the future He linked His presence to the breaking of the bread: "This is my body." That means: this is I Myself. At the same time He proclaimed that a new covenant would be established in and through His sacrificial death. Drinking the cup would mean to be admitted into this covenant and there to be regenerated.

There is a central concordance between this view and the view of St. Paul. Also here the communion with Christ is the main idea of the Eucharist. When St. Paul speaks of the remembrance—" do this in remembrance of me "—remembrance does not mean only a solemn reminder of Christ's sacrifice and death; it means also His presence in the cultus. This point of view is most strongly emphasized where the breaking of the bread is characterized as " communion of the body of Christ ". "The bread which we break, is it not the communion of the Body of Christ? For we being many are one bread and one body; for we are all partakers of that one bread " (1 Cor. x, 16-17). The communion with the living Christ is the soul of the Eucharist. However, it must be added that the view of His presence at the same time has an eschatological character. The eschatological perspective we find as well in the words of Jesus Himself as of St. Paul. "Truly I say to you, I shall not drink again of the fruit of the vine until that day when I drink it new in the Kingdom of God " (Mark xiv, 25). "For as often as ye eat this bread and drink this cup, ye do show the Lord's death till He come " (1 Cor. xi, 26).

The Holy Communion is, in the light of the New Testament, the Sacrament not only of the suffering Love, but also of the victorious Love of Christ. Through this Sacrament He realizes His victorious work of the resurrection in His Body, the Church. This view of the New Testament may be characterized as a very realistic one, because all here depends upon the action of Christ Himself. The view is neither magical nor only spiritualistic-symbolic, but sacramental. Certainly the Holy Communion is a mystery. But this mystery is nothing other than the mystery of the Gospel as a whole: that into this kingdom of death God has sent Him who is the Prince of Life, and that He has called us to be *one* with Him and to share in His Life.

VIII THE MINISTRY OF RECONCILIATION

According to the New Testament, the Ministry of the Church also belongs to the constitutive elements of the Church. The Ministry has its foundation in the mandate of Christ and is a necessary instrument for the edification of the Church through the Gospel and the Sacraments. Thus it appears as a Ministry of reconciliation. The biblical view of the Ministry will be obscured if the Ministry is interpreted either in a mechanical or in a subjective way.

In the New Testament the Ministry is inseparably connected with the Church. Having its origin in the mandate of Christ, it is a divine mission. The task of the Ministry is to serve Christ by serving the Church in her endeavours to penetrate the human world as deeply and as widely as possible. In this work the Ministry possesses authority, given by Christ, but this authority is not a personal authority, only an authority of service.

Everywhere in the New Testament it is emphasized that the Ministry has a divine mandate. The Lord says of His messengers: "As thou hast sent me into the world, even so have I also sent them into the world" (John xvii, 18). The messengers receive power to forgive sins in the name of the Lord (Matt. xviii, 18, cf. Matt. xvi, 19 and John xx, 22-3), but their authority is not their own. They are completely dependent on Christ, they are His instruments and servants (Matt. xx, 26-8; Matt. x, 40). Listening to St. Paul we find that he most strongly emphasizes the divine mandate that he has received, but also that he does not consider his authority as a personal authority; he himself is nothing but a servant (1 Cor. iii, 5 and iv, 1). His confidence comes from God (2 Cor. iii, 5, cf. 2 Cor. iv, 1). The Ministry can serve the Church only by wholly and entirely serving Christ (Gal. i, 10). The centre of the Ministry is reconciliation. Reconciliation claims the Ministry inasmuch as the victory of the reconciliation must be realized in fighting against the evil forces of destruction. The messengers know that in this fight no human power can accomplish anything; they know that Christ is the Victor, and that His messengers are allowed to go out in His name and with His authority.

As we have seen, the New Testament most strongly emphasizes the Ministry as a divine mandate. As Jesus sent out the apostles, so new messengers must be sent to succeed them. Then, from the biblical point of view, the most important thing as regards the legitimacy of the Ministry is undoubtedly that the message is really the apostolic message, that the Gospel is preached just as it is and not in false reinterpretations, and further that the Sacraments are administered according to Christ's will, and as instituted by Him.

Finally, service in the Church is obviously not confined to the Ministry. In fact, all the members of the Church are called to be servants in different ways. It is not possible to be a Christian without being a servant. However, that service which in the New Testament is connected with the word *diakonia* must specially be mentioned. When the Word and the Sacraments are active, action must follow. Service in love is and must be characteristic of the Church. One of the most important tasks of the Church at all times is therefore to give this service a position that adequately corresponds to its importance.

IX   THE NEW TESTAMENT AND THE UNITY OF THE CHURCH

For the New Testament the oneness of the Church is self-evident. Because the Church is the Body of Christ there can be but *one* Church. The unity is described as a unity in Christ or in the Spirit. St. Paul speaks about "one Body and one Spirit . . . one Lord, one faith, one baptism, one God and Father of all" (Eph. iv, 4-5).

This unity is a reality. But at the same time the New Testament very openly speaks of divisions and antagonisms which are a menace to unity. Repeatedly we find in the New Testament exhortations to maintain and realize unity. Christ's prayer is "that they all may be one" (John xvii, 21). St. Paul appeals to the Corinthians that "there be no dissensions among you", "Is Christ divided?" (1 Cor. i, 10 and 13), and he exhorts the Ephesians to be eager to maintain "the unity of the Spirit in the bond of peace" (Eph. iv, 3).

Considering the conditions and manifestations of unity according to the New Testament, we must emphasize that unity is not uniformity—neither uniformity of doctrine, nor uniformity of organization and orders, nor uniformity of life and religious experience.

Undoubtedly the basis of unity is to be found in the message of Christ as it appears in the Divine Word and in the Sacraments. There is no doubt that the New Testament considers this message as the foundation of the Church, without which the Church cannot exist, and therefore also as the basis of unity. But that does not mean uniformity of doctrine or theology. Obviously there are varieties of doctrine in the New Testament. The theology of St. John is not quite the same as the theology of St. Paul, nor the theology of the Epistle to the Hebrews. Nevertheless, in spite of the variety, the message is one and the same, a unity in variety.

Approaching the question of order and organization, here also we find unity in variety. The backbone of the organization is the apostolic Ministry as a divine institution on behalf of the Word and the Sacraments. Inasmuch as the Ministry is a true servant of the divine message, it represents the unity of the Church. However, we do not find any uniformity of order and organization. Obviously there are considerable differences in different parts of the Early Church. It would be wrong to consider the statements of the New Testament concerning questions of organization as fixed laws of the Church, valid for all ages and generations. The biblical view is characterized by firmness as well as by elasticity. Both are indispensable in the life of the Church. Also as regards elasticity, the principle of organization must be: the best means of serving the divine message which is the creative factor in the Church.

Finally, the unity of the Church is not uniformity of life. It is not based upon subjective experiences. The Church is not a union of individual Christians having the same religious experiences. Certainly the gift given to Christians in and through the Church is one and the same: salvation, the " new life ". But the New Testament shows us that this does not lead to uniformity of religious life. On the contrary, just as the light shining through a prism appears in different colours, so the gift of salvation appears in different human experiences and forms. A unity based on subjective experiences and qualifications must break. It cannot but lead to repeated divisions. The true basis of unity is not a subjective but an objective one: Christ acting through the Word and the Sacraments. The Church is not a closed society of specially qualified and " pure " members. The Church reaches as far as the power of Christ and His life-giving

Spirit is active in human souls. It is always a Church in the making, and its boundaries are always being re-defined.

.   .   .   .

We have here considered some features of the biblical view of the Church. In all endeavours to attain deeper unity it must be a help to return to the Bible. Not because we shall find there fixed rules concerning unity: the Bible is not a law for the Church. But there are other important reasons. First, the aim of the ecumenical movement is primarily a renewal of the Church, and no renewal has at any time taken place in the Church without help from the Bible. Secondly, the constitution of the Church is once and for all given and elucidated in the Bible. Thirdly, the Bible is the common ground of all Christians, and theology—as far as it is truly biblical—will undoubtedly promote Christian unity. We turn to the Bible, because the basis of Christian unity can only be the truth.

2

THE CHURCH OF THE NEW TESTAMENT

by Clarence T. Craig

WHEN the man of to-day hears the word "church", it awakens in his mind a wide variety of images. Some think at once of a *building*, ornate or simple, where the worship of God is celebrated. But the early Christians were groups without legal rights to possess institutional property. Amid the ruins of war-torn cities many modern Christians are discovering anew that the Church is not made of stone or brick. The living stones of the true Temple of God are those who worship Him in Spirit and in truth.

Others think of a denominational or territorial body. There are Methodists and Lutherans; Eastern Orthodox and Baptists; the Church of England and of Sweden. All of these names would have been equally strange to the first Christians. More than that, since the Church was by definition the people of God, there could not possibly be more than one. There could not be a Jewish church and a Gentile church, or a Macedonian church and a Judean. Christ had broken down the dividing wall of hostility and made of the different peoples one new man (Eph. ii, 14). In Christ all human distinctions were abolished (Col. iii, 11-12). As there was one God and one Lord and one faith and one baptism, there could only be one Church (Eph. iv, 4-5; i, 23; ii, 16).

Others think of a congregation of like-minded men and women who band themselves together to worship God in the way they choose. Of course the New Testament can use the word for the Christians living in one place (1 Cor. iv, 17), and even for small house communities (Rom. xvi, 5). But these were not groups which had been formed according to the pattern of other social clubs and religious societies. Believers had been called out by God, called into a society which He had created. They were the Elect, the Chosen. This was not their own doing, but it rested in the purpose of God Who sought a People for Himself.

I

If we are to understand the nature of the Church we must begin with the Old Testament. According to Acts vii, 38 there was already a church in the wilderness when God redeemed His people out of Egypt. Terms like new Israel and "Israel of God" would be pointless except against the background of a nation which had been so conceived as the people of God (Gal. vi, 16). If Christians were the "true circumcision" (Phil. iii, 3) and the "real sons of Abraham" (Rom. iv, 16; Gal. vi, 16) this Old Testament background is presupposed. A people of a New Covenant presupposed an Old Covenant. The Greek word *ekklesia* had no special religious connotation, as its use within the New Testament for a political assembly shows (Acts xix, 32, 39-40). It had acquired such significance because of its use in the Septuagint to translate the Hebrew *Qahal*. This was the term for the people of Israel, called out in solemn assembly, or ideally considered as such.

Throughout the Old Testament there is the conception of a People that God has chosen. The Hebrews looked back to Abraham as the one with whom God had made a covenant which would extend to his descendants (Gen. xv, 18; xvii, 7-8). He was the God Who had brought them up out of slavery in Egypt (Amos iii, 1; Hosea xi, 1; xiii, 4; 1 Kings viii, 51 *et passim*) and they were the People whom He had formed for Himself (Isaiah xliii, 21). His law had been revealed to Moses on the Mount (Ex. xxiv, 7-8), and this called for righteousness and the exclusive worship of the one God (Deut. vi, 13-15). They were to be a holy nation, a cult community (Ex. xix, 6; Ps. xcv, 6-7). Election involved responsibility for Israel rather than special privilege (Amos iii, 2). Over and over again the prophets censured Israel for her faithlessness (Isaiah i, 3-4; Hosea v, 3-5). The disasters which befell her were not historical misfortunes but the judgment of God (Micah i, 6; Amos iii, 6). Yet they looked forward to a coming act of redemption when His People would enjoy the full salvation of God (Isaiah ii, 2-4; ix, 2-7). The noblest spirits did not restrict this to Jews alone, but insisted that God wanted Israel to be a light to the nations of the world (Isaiah xlv, 22; xlix, 6; Zech. viii, 2off.) Yet even here, God's relation was not with isolated individuals, but with a People whom He had chosen.

When the word *ekklesia* is used in the New Testament it is with conscious reference to this Old Testament conception. One can hardly say, therefore, that Jesus founded the Church. The truth rather is that He redeemed the Church. For centuries there had been a people who looked upon themselves as set apart for God. When Christians applied the term *ekklesia* to themselves they re-defined the People of God in terms of the new acts of God for their redemption. It was not to be identified with Israel after the flesh, but with individuals from every tribe, nation, people, and tongue (Rev. vii, 9, etc.). Its adherents were not those who were strictly loyal to Torah, for Christ was the end of the law (Rom. x, 4). Its centre was not in a Temple where sacrifices were continually offered, but in Christ Who had died for their sins and been raised by God from the dead (1 Cor. xv, 3ff.). Though membership in the People of God was determined by different criteria, the basic conception of a Church goes back to the Old Testament. The true Remnant about which the prophets had spoken, had found fulfilment in the Christian community.

II

The gospels clearly indicate that the central message of Jesus did not deal with the Church. It was concerned with *the kingdom of God* and the repentance which was necessary if men should enter it by the gracious mercy of God (Mark i, 14-15). Jesus announced the nearness of the kingdom of God, a message which gave tremendous urgency to His ethical demands. A crisis was at hand; men must stand ready to pay any price to enter God's kingdom (Luke xiv, 25-33). Its approaching consummation meant the resurrection and the judgment, in other words, God's salvation.

But the message of Jesus did not deal exclusively with future events. The rule of God was already *present in His own ministry*. His healings and especially the demon exorcisms were evidence of the dawning powers of the new age (Matt. xii, 28). For those who had eyes to see, the mysterious presence of the kingdom of God was already manifest. The salvation of God had already appeared in the gracious work of Jesus (Matt. xi, 2-6). To reject Him was to refuse that salvation, for Jesus embodied the kingdom in His own person (Mark viii, 38).

Most startling was His announcement concerning *those who would enter* the kingdom when it should come in its fulness. It would not be for the rich but for the poor (Luke vi, 20ff.). It would not be for the wise scribes but for the little children and the childlike (Mark x, 14-15). It would not be for the righteous Pharisees but for the tax-collectors and sinners who were more ready to repent (Matt. xxi, 31). These were the groups which responded to the message of Jesus, and to them He gave assurance, "Fear not, little flock, for it is your Father's good pleasure to give you the kingdom" (Luke xii, 32).

Did the message of Jesus deal specifically with the Church? Biblical students are still far from agreement on the question. It is not to be solved simply by a discussion of the authenticity of the two passages in which Matthew employs *ekklesia* (Matt. xvi, 18; xviii, 17). It is the idea, not the term which is crucial. Neither 1 Peter nor the Gospel of John uses the word *ekklesia*, yet they are both documents which accord high importance to the Church. Certainly Jesus promised entrance to the kingdom of God to those who sincerely responded to His call. He gathered a group of disciples about Him. He did not form them into separate synagogues, but His disciples attended the appointed Jewish services. They had no separate cult acts during His life-time. Yet, since they were destined to enter the kingdom of God, were they not already the Church, whether gospel passages use that term or not?

Certainly in those who responded to the call of Jesus we find another part of the *background* for the Church. But many interpreters believe that it is inadmissible to apply the term with reference to that time. They believe that the passages which speak of the presence of the kingdom of God all refer to the activity of Jesus and that none relate this presence to the disciples. Other interpreters believe that this is quite accidental in the preservation of the tradition. They hold that since the Church is the anticipation in the present of the kingdom of God, those who were prepared to enter belonged to the Church even during the life-time of Jesus.

III

No one can doubt, however, that *the resurrection of Jesus* was central for the Church of the New Testament. Those who believed that God had raised Christ from the dead comprised the Church. God had vindicated His Messiah and the time of redemption had begun. With His resurrection the New Age was suddenly manifesting its power. Without that resurrection there was no full salvation because it was the ground for the resurrection of believers from the dead. We may say that the Christian Church was the community which had been constituted by God through the resurrection of Jesus.

A further indispensable mark of this community was its possession by the Holy Spirit. The gift of the Spirit had been promised for the end time. When the early Christians interpreted their ecstasy and joy and peace as caused by the Spirit, they meant that this had already come (Acts ii, 16ff.). The risen Christ had sent them the Spirit, the guarantee of His coming in glory. Though Christian tradition has followed Luke in dating the first experience of the Spirit fifty days after the crucifixion, John's Gospel puts this on the day of the resurrection (John xx, 22). That symbolizes the fact that belief in the resurrection and possession by the Spirit are twin signs for the identification of the Church.

The sharing by believers in the blessings of God was expressed through the word *koinonia*. Recent research has made it clear that when this word is followed by the genitive it should be translated not as " fellowship " but as " participation " or " sharing ".[1] The Church was a *koinonia* because its members participated in the same gifts. Sometimes the gift is Christ (1 Cor. i, 9); sometimes the Spirit (2 Cor. xiii, 14); sometimes God Himself (1 John i, 3). Since these were experiences which they shared in common there was a *koinonia* with one another (1 John 1, 7). This led to financial sharing within the brotherhood (Acts ii, 44-5; 2 Cor. viii, 9). Those who participated in the same spiritual blessings also shared their material resources. But there is no evidence that the word was ever used as a name for the group.

Yet many different terms were used. The author of 1 Peter addressed his readers as " a chosen race, a royal priesthood, a holy nation, God's own people " (1 Peter ii, 9-10). A whole series of Old Testament descriptions of Israel are thus applied

---

[1] J. Y. Campbell, " *koinonia* and its cognates in the New Testament ". *Journal of Biblical Literature*, LI, 352-80; H. Seeseman, *Der Begriff koinonia im N.T.* (1933); F. Hauck in *Theologisches Woerterbuch zum N.T.*, III, 804ff.

to the Church.   In the Gospel of John we read of the one flock
in which Christ's sheep are united.   Yet there are different
folds.   The farewell prayer of Christ is for the unity of all those
who believe through the word preached by the disciples (John
xvii, 21).   Believers are the branches of the one true vine (John
xv, 1-4).   They find their unity in Him, for apart from Him they
can do nothing.   To be in Christ, the crucified and risen Lord,
is to be in the Church.

IV

Entrance to the Church was by *faith and baptism*.   Faith was
more than accepting the truth of the Christian message.   It
involved repentance and a committal of life to the God Who had
raised Christ from the dead; it called for a dedication to Christ
as the Lord of their lives; it was possible through the gift which
God bestowed through His Spirit; it was the experience in which
the redeeming grace of God laid hold on the individual and
incorporated him into the body of Christ.   Jesus had called for
a similar faith, but during His ministry He had not baptized.
Very early, His Church practised baptism into the name of Jesus
as the seal of this experience.   It is not strange, therefore, that
water and the Spirit are associated over and over again with
entrance into the Christian life.

The life of this brotherhood in Christ was nourished by the
celebration of *the Lord's Supper*.   A common meal was the high
point of their worship.   It served to commemorate the Last
Supper which Jesus had celebrated with His disciples, when by
parabolic action and significant words He had pointed to His
redemptive death (1 Cor. xi, 23-5); the meal looked forward to
their reunion with Him in the banquet of the kingdom of God
(Mark xiv, 25).   But it likewise served to realize His presence as
the unseen host.   "The cup of blessing which we bless, is it not
a participation in the body of Christ?" (1 Cor. x, 16).   Or, as
another New Testament writer put it, Christ gave them in Himself nothing less than the bread of life (John vi, 48-51).

The New Testament Church was pre-eminently *a witnessing
community*, for its members were under obligation to proclaim
the Word of God and live in obedience to Him.   They were
stewards of the mysteries of God, ambassadors of His reconciliation (1 Cor. iv, 1; 2 Cor. v, 18f.).   The good news of His salva-

tion was not to be enjoyed in quiet satisfaction. The risen Christ had called them to be His witnesses to the end of the earth (Acts i, 8). Not only did an apostle like Paul respond to that summons. He rejoiced that his converts had sounded forth the Word of the Lord wherever they had gone (1 Thess. i, 8). The urgency of their missionary zeal was intensified because they were convinced that time was very short.

The New Testament Church looked forward eagerly to the speedy consummation of the kingdom of God. They had already experienced a real salvation in Christ. The man who was in Christ was a new creation and already walked in newness of life through the Spirit. The Fourth Gospel goes so far as to say that the believer already possessed eternal life through knowledge of the one true God in His Son. But the powers of evil had not yet been finally overcome. Believers lived in anticipation of the completion of God's reign. There was continuity between the Church on earth and the new age of God, but these are not the same. The city of the living God, the heavenly Jerusalem, lay beyond the coming resurrection (Heb. xii, 22). The Christ Who now ruled in His Church would ultimately reign as King of kings and Lord of lords (Rev. xix, 16).

v

Words are preserved in the gospels which indicate that there was contention over leadership within the Church (Mark ix, 34; x, 35-45). Jesus made it clear that there was no place for lordship among His disciples. Pre-eminence comes only through humble service. As He Himself had been the supreme Servant, those whom He sends forth as heralds of God's saving grace are to be servants of others. The touchstone of a truly *apostolic* ministry is to be found here. Minister and servant are alternative translations of the Greek.

The various ministries which developed in the early Church were due to differing endowments by the Spirit. All were gifts to His Church. Foremost among these was that of the *apostles* (1 Cor. xii, 28f.). An apostle was one who had seen the risen Lord (1 Cor. ix, 1); that distinction was not communicable to anyone else. The Twelve were included among these, for the risen Christ had appeared to that group (1 Cor. xv, 5). That number had been chosen by Jesus from His disciples with reference to the eschatological kingdom (Matt. xix, 28). Only twelve could sit on thrones judging the twelve tribes of Israel. But there were other apostles whom the risen Christ sent forth as missionaries and these were accorded the same authority (Acts xiv, 14; Rom. xvi, 7).

Working with the apostles were *prophets and teachers*, the other ministers of the Word. The preaching of the Gospel was the supreme function. In addition, there were those who possessed *gifts of healing* and who performed other services to the community. Since all believers shared in the priesthood and Christ was the great high priest in Heaven (1 Pet. ii, 5; Heb. iv, 14) there was no place in the New Testament for ministers who should bear the title of priest. There was need for men in various administrative capacities. In many places in the New Testament these bear no specific title (Heb. xiii, 7; 1 Thess. v, 12; 1 Cor. xvi, 15). Only once does Paul refer to bishops and deacons (Phil. i, 1). In the Acts of the Apostles, elders are mentioned in connection with some of the communities (Acts xiv, 23; xv, 6; xx, 17), and this term is used in other New Testament writings (1 Tim. v, 17; 1 Pet. v, 1; 2 John, 1). Ultimately the Church was to develop an administrative hierarchy of bishop, elders, and deacons, but this is not found within the New Testament, which prescribes no one particular pattern of administration.

Was there a single central authority within the primitive Church? How was their unity to find expression amid scattered communities? There is some evidence that Jerusalem tried to exercise a supervisory relationship over the rest of the churches (Acts viii, 14). It is clear that James, the brother of Jesus, held a unique position of leadership there (Acts xv, 13; Gal. ii, 12). As independent an apostle as Paul showed a surprising deference to James, and he raised an offering for the saints at Jerusalem even from poverty-stricken Macedonian churches (Rom. xv, 26). Among the Twelve, Peter was clearly the leader. Since he was the first to whom the risen Christ appeared there was real support for those who ascribed the primacy to him (1 Cor. xv, 5; Matt. xvi, 18). But the New Testament clearly indicates that he did not exercise ultimate authority (Gal. ii, 11f.). That rested only in the living Christ, Who is present where two or three are gathered together in His name (Matt. xviii, 20). The leadership of the Church depended then as now upon those whom He calls.

VI

The nature of the Church is not determined by any form of organization. It is determined by the relation of a community to Christ. He alone is the Head of the Church and He alone has the right to rule. This is set forth in the New Testament in three figures which express what the Church ought to be if it is the true Church.

First, it is a *building* built on the one foundation, Jesus Christ. Other foundation can no man lay than that which is laid in Jesus Christ (1 Cor. iii, 11). The various stones are fitted into that one building (1 Pet. ii, 5). This is not an outward structure but the *Temple* in which God dwells (1 Cor. iii, 16; 2 Cor. vi, 16; Eph. ii, 21) and of which He is the builder. The Temple at Jerusalem might be destroyed, but the new Temple which replaced it was the Church (John ii, 19). God did not dwell in a place but in a people, a people who rested on Christ as their foundation.

The second figure is that of the Church as *the Bride of Christ* (2 Cor. xi, 2; Rev. xix, 7). That symbolized two things, its obedience and its purity. The author of Ephesians did not think in terms of a democratic marriage or of a patriarchal home. Though we may not agree with the figure that is used we can agree upon the importance of the Church's obedience to Christ. Christ had cleansed the Church that she might be "holy and without blemish". "The saints" is one of the most frequent names for Christians in the New Testament; the conception is epitomized in the phrase of the creed, "I believe in the Holy Catholic Church". But this holiness did not mean that all the members of the Church were perfect individually. Many weeds were to be found among the wheat (Matt. xiii, 24-30), and our records of the apostolic Church bear eloquent testimony to the weakness and failure of the first followers of Jesus. But the Church in which we believe is the pure bride of Christ, the holy community of the People of God.

The most important of the figures is that of the *Body of Christ*. When in the Fourth Gospel it is said that the body of Christ will replace the temple which the Jews will destroy, this may refer to the Church as well as to the risen presence of Jesus

(John ii, 19). But it is Paul who develops the figure most fully, and it is with his application that one must be concerned in trying to understand its meaning. It is easy to repeat the phrase without taking the metaphor seriously. Though we may not think so realistically as a man of the first century, we may still find important teaching in this figure. If the Church is the Body of Christ it tells us three definite things about its nature.

(a) First, a body provides a vivid expression of *unity amid diversity* (1 Cor. xii, 12, 27; Rom. xii, 5). Paul elaborated this insight in the twelfth chapter of his first letter to Corinth. A body has many members and these have different functions. Yet it needs them all if it is to be truly a body. Modern ingenuity has gone far in supplying substitutes for hands and feet which have been lost in battle or by accident, but this only emphasizes how much we need them all. A body is a whole which needs all of its differing parts.

The bearing of this on the separativeness of our denominations and national churches should be obvious. Since the members are not alike, they dare not remain apart, or the wholeness of the body will not find expression. Only blind bigotry can make the intolerant claim that because the hand is not the eye therefore it is no part of the body. In the Creed we express our belief in the *Catholic* Church. Since that means *wholeness*, the true Church will find its unity not by uniformity but in the midst of diversity. This was certainly the case in the apostolic Church. It had place for a Paul, to whom Christ was the end of the law, and for Matthew, to whom Christ was a new law-giver. It included James with his moralism and John with his mysticism. If there could be place for such divergences in the first century, there should likewise be room within the Church of to-day for similar variety in expression. That inheres in the very nature of a body.

(b) A second function of every body is to be *the agency* for the visible expression of the soul or spirit. We should not be diverted by details of psychological terminology. All that is meant is that though the person is not identifiable with the body, he cannot be identified without it. This truth may become more vivid to us if we distinguish a body from a corpse and a ghost. A corpse weighs as much as the body, but it no longer expresses "the spirit of the departed". A ghost is a spirit which by definition has no effective embodiment in the world of time and space.

If the Church is the body of Christ, this recognizes the fact that He cannot be fully operative in our world as a disembodied spirit. His spirit must act through some bodily expression if its existence is to be manifest. The Church is the indispensable organ through which Christ makes His life effective in the world. Naturally God is not limited in the way that men are limited by their bodily organism. Certainly the risen Christ can never be completely contained within any ecclesiastical institution. But if the Church is the Body of Christ, it is where His Spirit is effective.

This figure should help us to identify the Church. If it is the Body of Christ no outward forms can guarantee the Church's presence. An institution may become a corpse from which the true spirit of Christ has departed. That possibility should not lead to charges against members of the Body whose polity and forms of worship differ from our own. It should awaken the deepest heart-searching within every branch of His Church. The real Body of Christ is the agency which incarnates His Spirit and incorporates His life.

(c) A third analogy is to be found in that a body is an *organism which develops by transformation from within*. A building may increase in size as separate bricks are laid on one another. But a body does not grow by adding fixed and separate parts. It grows as new material is taken up into the organism and made part of an interacting whole. When Paul called Christ "the head of the body", he may have thought of that part as direct- ing growth (Col. i, 18; Eph. iv, 15). Though our conceptions of biology are quite different, we may still appreciate what the New Testament was endeavouring to express. If the Church is the Body of Christ, He is the inner principle of growth. Growth does not come through the external addition of parts which remain unchanged, but through the inner transformation of these as believers are made new creatures in Him.

If the members thus become parts of one body, the result must follow that all are affected by what happens to any part. An injury to a man's arm has an effect on the whole organism. If the Church *is* the Body of Christ, it should be impossible for members in one part of the world to be afflicted without intense pain to the rest. Members that belong to the same body will suffer together and rejoice together (1 Cor. xii, 26). If this is not the case, would one not conclude that this member is either paralysed or is already cut off from the rest of the body?

The Church of the New Testament considered itself to be the heir of the promises of God in the Old Testament and the foretaste of a new humanity. It was the community of those who looked to Christ as their risen Lord and Saviour. He was the Rock upon which they were built and the Head into which they grew. It was a community marked by the gifts and the power of the Holy Spirit. Those who participated in these blessings shared with each other for they were part of the same body, the body of Christ. This community had been entrusted with the gospel of God's salvation, the word of His wisdom and power. Men and women entered this society on the call of God by faith and baptism. Their lives were strengthened as they partook of the Lord's Supper. Against that fellowship the powers of death have been without avail, for the struggling Church militant looks forward to the Church Triumphant which is the Kingdom of God.

3

THE CHURCH: HER NATURE AND TASK

by George Florovsky

I

IT is impossible to start with a formal definition of the Church.
For, strictly speaking, there is none which could claim any
doctrinal authority. None can be found in the Fathers nor
in the Schoolmen, nor even in St. Thomas Aquinas. No definition has been given by the Ecumenical Councils, nor by the
later Great Councils in the West, including those of Trent and
the Vatican. In the doctrinal summaries, drafted on various
occasions in the Eastern (Orthodox) church in the seventeenth
century and taken often (but wrongly) for the "symbolic books",
again no definition of the Church was given, except a reference
to the relevant clause of the Creed, followed by some comments.
This lack of formal definitions does not mean, however, a confusion of ideas or any obscurity of view. The Fathers did not
care so much for the *doctrine* of the Church precisely because
the glorious *reality* of the Church was open to their spiritual
vision. One does not define what is self-evident. This accounts
for the absence of a special chapter on the Church in all early
presentations of Christian doctrine: in Origen, in St. Gregory
of Nyssa, even in St. John of Damascus. Only some passing and
scattered remarks can be found even in the *Summa Theologica*
of Aquinas. The first systematic treatise on the Church was
composed in the West only in the late fifteenth century by the
Cardinal de Turrecremata (Rome 1489). "The Church existed
for about fifteen hundred years without reflecting upon its
nature and without attempting its clarification by a logical conception."[1]

The current definitions we find in our modern catechisms
and in the theological text-books are obviously of a late date.
Most of them were coined in the age of the Reformation, in the
spirit of confessional controversy, and for polemical purposes.
They were meant more to meet the needs of a particular age

[1] Bartmann, *Dogmatik*, Bk. II, para. 137.

than to articulate the free self-consciousness of the Church. No
wonder they prove to be inadequate and insufficient under the
changed conditions. They are, all of them, in an eminent sense
"situation-conditioned". And again they are theological, not
doctrinal, statements; they are merely tentative and provisional,
as it were only private opinions of theologians, however widely
(or even "commonly") they may have been accepted. They
belong more to the school than to the Church. There is no
proper teaching authority standing behind them, and therefore
these definitions cannot be regarded as binding, final or complete. Many modern scholars, both Roman and Orthodox, have
plainly stated that the Church itself has not yet defined its own
essence and nature. " Die Kirche selbst hat sich bis heute noch
nicht definiert," says Robert Grosche.[2] Some theologians go
even further and suggest that no definition of the Church is
possible.[3] In any case the true theology of the Church is still
im Werden, in the process of formation. The doctrine of the
Church has hardly passed its *pre*-theological phase.[4]

In our time, it seems, one has to get beyond the modern
theological disputes, to regain a wider historical perspective, to
recover the true "catholic mind", which would embrace the
whole of the historical experience of the Church in its pilgrimage
through the ages. One has to return from the school-room to
the worshipping Church and perhaps to change the school-dialect
of theology for the pictorial and metaphorical language of Scripture. The very nature of the Church can be rather depicted
and described than properly defined. And surely this can be
done only from within the Church. Probably even this description will be convincing only for those of the Church. The
Mystery is apprehended only by faith.

II

The Greek name *ekklesia* adopted by the primitive Christians
to denote the New Reality, in which they were aware they shared,
presumed and suggested a very definite conception of what the
Church really was. Adopted under an obvious influence of the
Septuagint use, this word stressed first of all the organic con-

---

[2] Robert Grosche, *Pilgernde Kirche*, Freiburg im Breisgau, 1938, p. 27.
[3] Sergius Bulgakov, *The Orthodox Church* (1935) p. 12; Stefan Zankow, *Das
Orthodoxe Christentum des Ostens*, Berlin 1928, p. 65; English translation by
Dr. Lowrie, 1929, p. 69f.
[4] See M. D. Koster, *Ecclesiologie im Werden*, Paderborn 1940.

tinuity of the two Covenants. The Christian existence was conceived in the sacred perspective of the Messianic preparation and fulfilment (Heb. i, 1-2). A very definite theology of history was thereby implied. The Church was the true Israel, the new Chosen People of God, "a chosen generation, a holy nation, a peculiar people" (1 Pet. ii, 9). Or rather, it was the faithful Remnant, selected out of the unresponsive People of old.[5] And all nations of the earth, Greeks and Barbarians, were to be co-opted and grafted into this new People of God by the call of God (this was the main theme of St. Paul in Romans and Galatians— cf. Ephesians ch. ii).

Already in the Old Testament the word *ekklesia* (a rendering in Greek of the Hebrew *Qahal*) did imply a special emphasis on the ultimate unity of the Chosen People, conceived as a sacred whole, and this unity was rooted more in the mystery of the divine election than in any "natural" features. This emphasis could only be confirmed by the supplementary influence of the Hellenistic use of the word *ekklesia* meaning usually an assembly of the sovereign people in a city, a general congregation of all regular citizens. Applied to the new Christian existence, the word kept its traditional connotation. The Church was both the People and the City. A special stress has been put on the organic unity of Christians.

Christianity from the very beginning existed as a corporate reality, as a community. To be Christian meant just to belong to the community. Nobody could be Christian by himself, as an isolated individual, but only together with "the brethren", in a "togetherness" with them. *Unus Christianus—nullus Christianus*. Personal conviction or even a rule of life still do not make one a Christian. Christian existence presumes and implies an incorporation, a membership in the community. This must be qualified at once: in the *Apostolic* community, i.e. in communion with the Twelve and their message. The Christian "community" was gathered and constituted by Jesus Himself "in the days of His flesh", and it was given by Him at least a provisional constitution by the election and the appointment of the Twelve, to whom He gave the name (or rather the title) of His "messengers" or "ambassadors".[6] For a "sending forth"

[5] Luke xii, 32: "*little flock*" seems to mean precisely the "remnant", recon-stituted and redeemed, and reconsecrated.
[6] See Luke vi, 13: "whom also *he named apostles*."

of the Twelve was not only a mission, but precisely a commission, for which they were invested with a "power" (Mark iii, 15; Matt. x, 1; Luke ix, 1). In any case as the appointed "witnesses" of the Lord (Luke xxiv, 48; Acts i, 8) the Twelve alone were entitled to secure the continuity both of the Christian message and of the community life. Therefore communion with the Apostles was a basic note of the primitive "Church of God" in Jerusalem (Acts ii, 42: *koinonia*).

Christianity means a "common life", a life in common. Christians have to regard themselves as "brethren" (in fact this was one of their first names), as members of one corporation, closely linked together. And therefore charity had to be the first mark and the first proof as well as the token of this fellowship. We are entitled to say: Christianity *is* a community, a corporation, a fellowship, a brotherhood, a "society", *coetus fidelium*. And surely, as a first approximation, such a description could be of help. But obviously it requires a further qualification, and something crucial is missing here. One has to ask: in what exactly this unity and togetherness of the many is based and rooted? what is the power that brings many together and joins them one with another? Is this merely a social instinct, some power of social cohesion, an impetus of mutual affection, or any other natural attraction? Is this unity based simply on unanimity, on identity of views or convictions? Briefly, is the Christian Community, the Church, merely a human society, a society of men? Surely, the clear evidence of the New Testament takes us far beyond this purely human level. Christians are united not only among themselves, but first of all they *are one—in Christ*, and only this communion *with* Christ makes the communion of men first possible—*in* Him. The centre of unity *is the Lord* and the power that effects and enacts the unity *is the Spirit*. Christians are constituted into this unity by divine design; by the Will and Power of God. Their unity comes from above. They are one only in Christ, as those who had been born anew in Him, "rooted and built up in Him" (Col. ii, 7), who by One Spirit have been "baptized into One Body" (1 Cor. xii, 13). The Church of God has been established and constituted by God through Jesus Christ, Our Lord: "she is His own creation by water and the word". Thus there is no human society, but rather a "Divine Society", not a secular community, which would have been still "of this world", still commensurable with other human groups, but a sacred community, which is intrinsically "not of this world", not even of "this aeon", but of the "aeon to come".

Moreover, Christ Himself belongs to this community, as its Head, not only as its Lord or Master. Christ is not above or outside of the Church. The Church *is in Him*. The Church is not merely a community of those who believe in Christ and walk in His steps or in His commandments. She is a community of those who abide and dwell in Him, and in whom He Himself is abiding and dwelling by the Spirit. Christians are set apart, "born anew" and re-created, they are given not only a new pattern of life, but rather a new principle: the new Life in the Lord by the Spirit. They are a "peculiar People", "the People of God's own possession". The point is that the Christian Community, the *ekklesia*, is a *sacramental community*: *communio in sacris*, a "fellowship in holy things", i.e. in the Holy Spirit, or even *communio sanctorum* (*sanctorum* being taken as neuter rather than masculine—perhaps that was the original meaning of the phrase). The unity of the Church is effected through the sacraments: Baptism and the Eucharist are the two "social sacraments" of the Church, and in them the true meaning of Christian "togetherness" is continually revealed and sealed. Or even more emphatically, the sacraments constitute the Church. Only in the sacraments does the Christian Community pass beyond the purely human measure and become the Church. Therefore "the right administration of the sacraments" belongs to the essence of the Church (to her *esse*). Sacraments must be "worthily" received indeed, therefore they cannot be separated or divorced from the inner effort and spiritual attitude of believers. Baptism is to be preceded by repentance and faith. A personal relation between an aspirant and his Lord must be first established by the hearing and the receiving of the Word, of the message of salvation. And again an oath of allegiance to God and His Christ is a pre-requisite and indispensable condition of the administration of the sacrament (the first meaning of the word *sacramentum* was precisely "the (military) oath"). A catechumen is already "enrolled" among the brethren on the basis of his faith. Again, the baptismal gift is appropriated, received and kept, by faith and faithfulness, by the steadfast standing in the faith and the promises. And yet sacraments are not merely signs of a professed faith, but rather effective signs of the saving Grace—not only symbols of human aspiration and loyalty, but the outward symbols of the divine action. In them our human existence is linked to, or rather raised up to, the Divine Life, by the Spirit, the giver of life.

The Church as a whole is a *sacred* (or consecrated) community, distinguished thereby from " the (profane) world ". She is the *Holy Church*. St. Paul obviously uses the terms " Church " and " saints " as co-extensive and synonymous. It is remarkable that in the New Testament the name " saint " is almost exclusively used in the plural, saintliness being social in its intrinsic meaning. For the name refers not to any human achievement, but to a gift, to sanctification or consecration. Holiness comes from the Holy One, i.e. only from God. To be holy for a man means to share the Divine Life. Holiness is available to individuals only in the community, or rather in the " fellowship of the Holy Ghost ". The " communion of saints " is a pleonasm. One can be a " saint " only in the communion.

Strictly speaking, the Messianic Community, gathered by Jesus the Christ, was not yet the Church, before His Passion and Resurrection, before " the promise of the Father " was sent upon it and it was " endued with the power from on high ", " baptized with the Holy Ghost " (cf. Luke xxiv, 49 and Acts i, 4-5), in the mystery of Pentecost. Before the victory of the Cross disclosed in the glorious Resurrection, it was still *sub umbraculo legis*. It was still the eve of the fulfilment. And Pentecost was there to witness to and to seal the victory of Christ. " The power from on high " has entered into history. The " new aeon " has been truly disclosed and started. And the sacramental life of the Church is the continuation of Pentecost.

The descent of the Spirit was a supreme revelation. Once and for ever, in the " dreadful and inscrutable mystery " of Pentecost, the Spirit-Comforter enters the world in which He was not yet present in such manner as now He begins to dwell and to abide. An abundant spring of living water is disclosed on that day, here on earth, in the world which had been already redeemed and reconciled with God by the Crucified and Risen Lord. The Kingdom comes, for the Holy Spirit is the Kingdom.[7] But the

---

[7] Cf. St. Gregory of Nyssa, *De oratione Dominica*, 3, MG, XLIV, c. 115f.-116o. (Note: In these footnotes, MG and ML refer to *Migne*, series *Greek* and *Latin* respectively.)

"coming" of the Spirit depends upon the "going" of the Son (John xvi, 7). "Another Comforter" comes down to testify of the Son, to reveal His glory and to seal His victory (xv, 26; xvi, 7 and 14). Indeed in the Holy Spirit the Glorified Lord Himself comes back or returns to His flock to abide with them always (xiv, 18 and 28). . . . Pentecost was the mystical consecration, the baptism of the whole Church (Acts i, 5). This fiery baptism was administered by the Lord: for He baptizes "with the Holy Spirit and with fire" (Matt. iii, 11 and Luke iii, 16). He has sent the Spirit from the Father, as a pledge in our hearts. The Holy Ghost is the spirit of adoption, in Christ Jesus, "the power of Christ" (2 Cor. xii, 9). By the Spirit we recognize and we acknowledge that Jesus is the Lord (1 Cor. xii, 3). The work of the Spirit in believers is precisely their incorporation into Christ, their baptism into one body (xii, 13), even the body of Christ. As St. Athanasius puts it: "being given drink of the Spirit, we drink Christ". For the Rock was Christ.[8]

By the Spirit Christians are united with Christ, are united in Him, are constituted into His Body. *One body*, that of Christ: this excellent analogy used by St. Paul in various contexts, when depicting the mystery of Christian existence, is at the same time the best witness to the intimate experience of the Apostolic Church. By no means was it an accidental metaphorical image: it was rather a summary of faith and experience. With St. Paul the main emphasis was always on the intimate union of the faithful with the Lord, on their sharing in His fulness. As St. John Chrysostom has pointed out, commenting on Col. iii, 4, in all his writings St. Paul was endeavouring to prove that the believers "are in communion with Him in all things" and "precisely to show this union does he speak of the Head and the body".[9] It is highly probable that the term was suggested by the Eucharistic experience (cf. 1 Cor. x, 17), and was deliberately used to suggest its sacramental connotation. The Church of Christ is one in the Eucharist, for the Eucharist is Christ Himself, and He *sacramentally* abides in the Church, which is His Body. The Church is a body indeed, *an organism*, much more than a society or a corporation. And perhaps an "organism" is the best modern rendering of the term *to soma*, as used by St. Paul.

[8] S. Athan. Alex., *Epist, 1 ad Serapionem*, MG, XXVI, 576.
[9] St. John Chrysostom, in *Coloss. hom. VII*, MG, LXII, col. 375.

D

Still more, the Church is the body *of Christ* and His "fulness". *Body* and *fulness* (*to soma* and *to pleroma*)—these two terms are correlative and closely linked together in St. Paul's mind, one explaining the other: "which is His body, the fulness of Him Who all in all is being fulfilled" (Eph. i, 23). The Church is the Body of Christ because it is His *complement*. St. John Chrysostom commends the Pauline idea just in this sense. "The Church is the complement of Christ in the same manner in which the head completes the body and the body is completed by the head." Christ is not alone. "He has prepared the whole race in common to follow Him, to cling to Him, to accompany His train." Chrysostom insists, "Observe how he (i.e. St. Paul) introduces Him as having need of all the members. This means that only then will the Head be filled up, when the Body is rendered perfect, when we are all together, co-united and knit together."[10]   In other words, the Church is the extension and the "fulness" of the Holy Incarnation, or rather of the Incarnate life of the Son, "with all that for our sakes was brought to pass, the Cross and tomb, the Resurrection the third day, the Ascension into Heaven, the sitting on the right hand" (Liturgy of St. John Chrysostom, Prayer of Consecration).

The Incarnation is being completed in the Church. And, in a certain sense, the Church is Christ Himself, in His all-embracing plenitude (cf. 1 Cor. xii, 12). This identification has been suggested and vindicated by St. Augustine: "*Non solum nos Christianos factos esse, sed Christum.*" For if He is the Head, we are the members: the whole man is He and we—"*totus homo, ille et nos—Christus et Ecclesia*". And again: "For Christ is not simply in the head and not in the body (only), but Christ is entire in the head and body"—"*non enim Christus in capite et non in corpore, sed Christus totus in capite et in corpore.*"[11]   This term *totus Christus*[12] occurs in St. Augustine again and again, this is his basic and favourite idea, suggested obviously by St. Paul. "When I speak of Christians in the plural, I understand one in the One Christ. Ye are therefore many, and ye are yet one: we are many and we are one"—"*cum plures Christianos appello, in uno Christo unum intelligo.*"[13]

[10] St. John Chrysostom in *Ephes. hom. III*, MG, LXII, col. 29.
[11] St. Augustine in *Evangelium Joannis tract, XXI, 8*, ML, XXXV, col. 1568; cf. St. John Chrysostom in *1 Cor. hom. XXX*, MG, LXI, col. 279-283.
[12] St. Augustine in *Ev. Joannis tr. XXVIII*, c. 1622.
[13] St. Augustine in *Ps. CXXVII, 3*, ML, XXXVII, col. 1679.

"For our Lord Jesus is not only in Himself, but in us also "—
" *Dominus enim Jesus non solum in se, sed et in nobis.*"[14] " One
Man up to the end of the ages "—" *Unus homo usque ad finem
saeculi extenditur.*"[15]

The main contention of all these utterances is obvious. Christians are incorporated into Christ and Christ abides in them—
this intimate union constitutes the mystery of the Church. The
Church is, as it were, the place and the mode of the redeeming
presence of the Risen Lord in the redeemed world. " The Body
of Christ is Christ Himself. The Church is Christ, as after His
Resurrection He is present with us and encounters us here
on earth."[16] And in this sense one can say: Christ is the
Church. " *Ipse enim est Ecclesia, per sacramentum corporis
sui in se universam eam continens.*"[17] Or in the words of
Karl Adam: " Christ, the Lord, is the proper Ego of the
Church."[18]

The Church is the unity of charismatic life. The source of
this unity is hidden in the sacrament of the Lord's Supper and
in the mystery of Pentecost. And Pentecost is continued and
made permanent in the Church by means of the Apostolic Succession. It is not merely, as it were, the canonic skeleton of
the Church. Ministry (or "hierarchy") itself is primarily a
charismatic principle, a "ministry of the sacraments", or "a
divine oeconomia". Ministry is not only a *canonical* commission, it belongs not only to the *institutional* fabric of the Church
—it is rather an indispensable constitutional or *structural*
feature, just in so far as the Church is a body, an organism.
Ministers are not, as it were, " commissioned officers " of the community, not only leaders or delegates of the " multitudes ", of the
" people " or " congregation "—they are acting not only *in
persona ecclesiae.* They are acting primarily *in persona Christi.*
They are " representatives " of Christ Himself, not of believers,
and in them and through them, the Head of the Body, the only
High Priest of the New Covenant, is performing, continuing and
accomplishing His eternal pastoral and priestly office. He is
Himself the only true Minister of the Church. All others are

[14] St. Augustine in *Ps. XC enarr. 1*, 9, ML, XXXVII, col. 1157.
[15] St. Augustine in *Ps. LXXXV, 5*, ML, XXXVII, col. 1083.
[16] A. Nygren, *Corpus Christi*, in *En Bok om Kyrkan, av Svenska teologer*, Lund, 1943, p. 20.
[17] St. Hilary in *Ps. CXXV, 6*, ML, IX, c. 688.
[18] Karl Adam, *Das Wesen des Katholizismus*, 4 Ausgabe, 1927, p. 24.

but stewards of His mysteries. They are standing *for* Him, *before* the community—and just because the Body is one only in its Head, is brought together and into unity by Him and in Him, the Ministry in the Church is primarily the Ministry of unity. In the Ministry the organic unity of the Body is not only represented or exhibited, but rather rooted, without any prejudice to the "equality" of the believers, just as the "equality" of the cells of an organism is not destroyed by their structural differentiation: all cells are equal as such, and yet differentiated by their functions, and again this differentiation serves the unity, enables this organic unity to become more comprehensive and more intimate. The unity of every local congregation springs from the unity in the Eucharistic meal. And it is as the celebrant of the Eucharist that the priest is the minister and the builder of Church unity. But there is another and higher office: to secure the universal and catholic unity of the whole Church in space and time. This is the episcopal office and function. On the one hand, the Bishop has an authority to ordain, and again this is not only a jurisdictional privilege, but precisely a power of sacramental action beyond that possessed by the priest. Thus the Bishop as "ordainer" is the builder of Church unity on a wider scale. The Last Supper and Pentecost are inseparably linked to one another. The Spirit Comforter descends when the Son has been glorified in His death and resurrection. But still they are two sacraments (or mysteries) which cannot be merged into one another. In the same way the priesthood and the episcopate differ from one another. In the episcopacy Pentecost becomes universal and continuous, in the undivided episcopate of the Church (*episcopatus unus* of St. Cyprian) the unity in space is secured. On the other hand, through its bishop, or rather in its bishop, every particular or local Church is included in the catholic fulness of the Church, is linked with the past and with all ages. In its bishop every single Church outgrows and transcends its own limits and is organically united with the others. The Apostolic Succession is not so much the canonical as the mystical foundation of Church unity. It is something other than a safeguard of historical continuity or of administrative cohesion. It is an ultimate means to keep the mystical identity of the Body through the ages. But, of course, Ministry is never detached from the Body. It is in the Body, belongs to its structure. And ministerial gifts are given inside the Church (cf. 1 Cor. xii).

The Pauline conception of the Body of Christ was taken up and variously commented on by the Fathers, both in the East and in the West, and then was rather forgotten.[19] It is high time now to return to this experience of the early Church which may provide us with a solid ground for a modern theological synthesis. Some other similes and metaphors were used by St. Paul and elsewhere in the New Testament, but much to the same purpose and effect: to stress the intimate and organic unity between Christ and those who are His. But, among all these various images, that of the Body is the most inclusive and impressive, is the most emphatic expression of the basic vision.[20] Of course, no analogy is to be pressed too far or over-emphasized. The idea of an organism, when used of the Church, has its own limitations. On the one hand, the Church is composed of human personalities, which never can be regarded merely as elements or cells of the whole, because each is in direct and immediate union with Christ and His Father—the personal is not to be sacrificed or dissolved in the corporate, Christian " togetherness " must not degenerate into impersonalism. The idea of the organism must be supplemented by the idea of a symphony of personalities, in which the mystery of the Holy Trinity is reflected (cf. John xvii, 21 and 23), and this is the core of the conception of "catholicity" ("sobornost").[21] This is the chief reason why we should prefer a christological orientation in the theology of the Church rather than a pneumatological.[22] For, on the other hand, the Church, as a whole, has her *personal centre* only in Christ, she is not an incarnation of the Holy Ghost, nor is she merely a Spirit-bearing community, but

[19] See E. Mersch, S.J., *Le Corps Mystique du Christ, Études de Theologie Historique*, 2 vols., 2nd edition, Louvain 1936; cf. also the recent Encyclical *Mystici Corporis Christi*.

[20] The image of the Bride and her mystical marriage with Christ (Eph. v, 23f.) expresses the intimate union. Even the image of the House built of many stones, the corner stone being Christ (Eph. ii, 20f.; cf. 1 Pet. ii, 6), tends to the same purpose: many are becoming one, and the tower appears as it were built or one stone (cf. Hermas, *Shepherd*, Vis. III, ii, 6, 8). And again "the People of God" is to be regarded as an organic whole. There is no reason whatever to be troubled by the variety of vocabularies used. The main idea and contention 1 obviously the same in all cases.

[21] Cf. George Florovsky, "Sobornost, The Catholicity of the Church", in *The Church of God, an Anglo-Russian Symposium*, ed. by E. L. Mascall, London 1935.

[22] Such as in Khomiakov or in Moehler's *Die Einheit in der Kirche*.

precisely the Body of Christ, the Incarnate Lord. This saves us from impersonalism without committing us to any humanistic personification. Christ the Lord is the only Head and the only Master of the Church. "In Him the whole structure is closely fitted together and grows into a temple holy in the Lord; in Him you too are being built together into a dwelling-place for God in the Spirit" (Eph. ii, 21-22, Bp. Challoner's version).

The Christology of the Church does not lead us into the misty clouds of vain speculations or dreamy mysticism. On the contrary, it secures the only solid and positive ground for proper theological research. The doctrine of the Church finds thereby its proper and organic place in the general scheme of the Divine Oeconomia of salvation. For we have indeed still to search for a comprehensive vision of the mystery of our salvation, of the salvation of the world.

One last distinction is to be made. The Church is still *in statu viae* and yet it is already *in statu patriae*. It has, as it were, a double life, both in heaven and on earth.[23] The Church is a visible historical society, and the same is the Body of Christ. It is both the Church of the redeemed, and the Church of the miserable sinners—both at once. On the historical level no *final* goal has yet been attained. But the *ultimate* reality has been disclosed and revealed. This ultimate reality is still at hand, is truly available, in spite of the historical imperfection, though but in provisional forms. For the Church is a sacramental society. *Sacramental* means no less than "*eschatological*". *To eschaton* does not mean primarily *final*, in the temporal series of events; it means rather *ultimate* (decisive); and the ultimate is being realized within the stress of historical happenings and events. What is "not of this world" is here "in this world", not abolishing this world, but giving to it a new meaning and a new value, "transvaluating" the world, as it were. Surely this is still only an anticipation, a "token" of the final consummation. Yet the Spirit abides in the Church. This constitutes the mystery of the Church: a visible "society" of frail men *is* an organism of the Divine Grace.[24]

---

[23] Cf. St. Augustine in *Evang. Joannis tract*, CXXIV, 5, ML, XXXV, c. 19f., 7.
[24] See Khomiakov's essay *On the Church*; English translation by W. J. Birkbeck, *Russia and the English Church* (first published 1895), ch. XXIII, pp. 193-222.

III

The primary task of the historical Church is the proclamation of the Gospel. To proclaim the Gospel means inevitably to pass a judgment upon the world. The Gospel itself is a judgment and a condemnation. It lays bare the sin of the world (cf. John iii, 19). There is an ultimate tension, a contrast and an opposition. The Gospel itself is "not of this world". It is a proclamation of another world "to come". The Church bears witness to the New Life, disclosed and revealed in Christ Jesus, the Lord and Saviour. This it does both by word and deed. The true proclamation of the Gospel would be precisely the practice of this New Life: to show faith by deeds (cf. Matt. v, 16).

The Church is more than a company of preachers, or a teaching society, or a missionary board. It has not only to invite people, but also to introduce them into this New Life, to which it bears witness. It is a missionary body indeed, and its mission-field is the whole world. But the aim of its missionary activity is not merely to convey to people certain convictions or ideas, not even to impose on them a definite discipline or a rule of life, but first of all to introduce them into the New Reality, to *convert* them, to bring them through their faith and repentance to Christ Himself, that they should be born anew in Him and into Him by water and the Spirit. Thus the ministry of the Word is completed in the ministry of the Sacraments.

"Conversion" is a fresh start, but it is only a start, to be followed by a long process of growth. The Church has to organize the new life of the converted. The Church has, as it were, to exhibit the new pattern of existence, the new mode of life, that of the "world to come". The Church is here, in this world, for its salvation. But just for this reason it has to oppose and to renounce "this" world. God claims the whole man, and the Church bears witness to this "totalitarian" claim of God revealed in Christ. The Christian has to be a "new creation". Therefore he cannot find a settled place for himself within the limits of the "old world". In this sense the Christian attitude is, as it were, always revolutionary with regard to the "old order" of "this world". Being "not of this world" the Church of Christ "in this world" can only be in permanent opposition, even if it claims only a reformation of the existing order. In any case, the change is to be radical and total.

Historical failures of the Church do not obscure the absolute and ultimate character of its challenge, to which it is committed by its very eschatological nature, and it constantly challenges itself.

Historical life and the task of the Church are an antinomy, and this antinomy can never be solved or overcome on a historical level. It is rather a permanent hint to what is "to come" hereafter. The antinomy is rooted in the practical alternative which the Church had to face from the very beginning of its historical pilgrimage. *Either* the Church was to be constituted as an exclusive and "totalitarian" society, endeavouring to satisfy all requirements of the believers, both "temporal" and "spiritual", paying no attention to the existing order and leaving nothing to the external world—it would have been an entire separation from the world, an ultimate flight out of it, and a radical denial of any external authority. *Or* the Church could attempt an inclusive Christianization of the world, subduing the whole of life to Christian rule and authority, to reform and to reorganize secular life on Christian principles, to build the Christian City. In the history of the Church we can trace both solutions: a flight to the desert and a construction of the Christian Empire. The first was practised not only in monasticism of various trends, but in many other Christian groups and denominations. The second was the main line taken by Christians, both in the West and in the East, up to the rise of militant secularism, but even in our days this solution has not lost its hold on many people. But on the whole, both proved unsuccessful. One has, however, to acknowledge the reality of their common problem and the truth of their common purpose. Christianity is not an individualistic religion and it is not only concerned for the "salvation of the soul". Christianity is the Church, i.e. a Community, the New People of God, leading its corporate life according to its peculiar principles. And this life cannot be split into departments, some of which might have been ruled by any other and heterogeneous principles. Spiritual leadership of the Church can hardly be reduced to an occasional guidance given to individuals or to groups living under conditions utterly uncongenial to the Church. The legitimacy of these conditions must be questioned first of all. The task of a

complete re-creation or re-shaping of the whole fabric of human
life cannot or must not be avoided or declined. One cannot
serve two Masters and a double allegiance is a poor solution.
Here the above-mentioned alternative inevitably comes in—
everything else would merely be an open compromise or a reduc-
tion of the ultimate and therefore *total* claims. *Either* Christians
ought to go out of the world, in which there is another Master
besides Christ (whatever name this other Master may bear:
Caesar or Mammon or any other) and in which the rule and the
goal of life are other than those set out in the Gospel—to go out
and to start a separate society. *Or* again Christians have to trans-
form the outer world, to make it the Kingdom of God as well,
and introduce the principles of the Gospel into secular legisla-
tion.

There is an inner consistency in both programmes. And
therefore the separation of the two ways is inevitable. Christians
seem compelled to take different ways. The unity of the Christian task is broken. An inner schism arises within the Church:
an abnormal separation between the monks (or the *élite* of the
initiated) and the lay-people (including clergy), which is far
more dangerous than the alleged " clericalization " of the
Church. In the last resort, however, it is only a symptom of the
ultimate antinomy. The problem simply has no historical solution. A true solution would transcend history, it belongs to the
" age to come ". In this age, on the historic plane, no constitutional principle can be given, but only a regulative one: a principle of discrimination, not a principle of construction.

For again each of the two programmes is self-contradictory.
There is an inherent *sectarian* temptation in the first: the
" catholic " and universal character of the Christian message and
purpose is here at least obscured and often deliberately denied,
the world is simply left out of sight. And all attempts at the
direct Christianization of the world, in the guise of a Christian
State or Empire, have only led to the more or less acute
secularization of Christianity itself.[25]

In our time nobody would consider it possible for everyone to
be converted to a universal monasticism or a realization of a
truly Christian, and universal, State. The Church remains

[25] For a more detailed treatment, see George Florovsky, *The Antinomies of
Christian History*, in the volume of Orthodox papers, published by the Study
Department of the World Council of Churches.

"in the world", as a heterogeneous body, and the tension is stronger than it has ever been; the ambiguity of the situation is painfully felt by everyone in the Church. A practical programme for the present age can be deduced only from a restored understanding of the nature and essence of the Church. And the failure of all Utopian expectations cannot obscure the Christian hope: the King has come, the Lord Jesus, and His Kingdom is to come.

4

ONE, HOLY, CATHOLIC, APOSTOLIC CHURCH

by John A. F. Gregg

I

THE Church is the extension in time and space of the Incarnate Word of God, crucified, ascended, glorified, operating among men through the indwelling in them of His Holy Spirit, Who mediates to it His Victorious Life. Thus, although the Church is visible and tangible, it is a supernatural corporation. Its life is on earth, but its citizenship is in heaven. Its habitat is this globe and the affairs of men are its concern, but the dwelling-place of its spirit is the eternal world. It has here no continuing city; it seeks a city which lies beyond.

The reason for this is found in the constitution of its being. As the Church of the Ascended Christ Whose Body it is, it is no self-constituted Society of like-minded seekers after ideal truth or of admirers of the prophet Jesus; it is a Society founded and constituted by an invisible Head in Whom resides all its vitality and apart from Whom it can do nothing. The distinguishing and confessed characteristic of its being lies in given-ness. "When He ascended up on high, He gave gifts unto men." Christ is its life, its hope, the secret of that revival and restoration of which, because of the fallibility of its human element, it stands in permanent need. This relationship is no mere subjective loyalty, resting on its members' faith and trust (although both are needed). The glorified Christ is the objective, constitutive Reality, without Whom its entire corporate existence would fall to the ground.

The relationship existing between the Head and the members of the Body is on the one hand of a personal and individual kind (though space does not permit us to dwell on it here), and on the other hand of a corporate and comprehensive kind. Various metaphors are employed which seek to suggest the closeness and the permanence of the latter.

(1) The Church is the Bride of Christ, bought with His

Blood, liberated from sin by the power of His Cross and quick-ened by His Life.

(2) The Church is His Body, its many members constituting the fulness of Him, its Head, Who all in all is being fulfilled.

(3) The Church is to Christ as the vine-branches are to the vine-stem. They can bear fruit only as they abide in Him.

(4) The Church is the flock of the Good Shepherd. This gracious and mystical relationship with the heavenly Bishop of our souls is postulated through the whole teaching of the Apostolic writings and underlies the witness of the Constantino-politan Creed to the One Holy Catholic and Apostolic Church.

Piety is very ready to think of the relationship to Christ in individualistic terms, drawn from or even justified by, such scriptural passages as Psalm xxiii. But such pictures as those specified above, and such a picture as that of the spiritual Temple, a fabric compacted out of countless living stones, force us to recognize that personal devotion to Christ must find its place side by side with the broader and more exacting love of the brethren. There is thus a deep truth underlying the appar-ently repellent *Extra ecclesiam nulla salus.*

For although when we study the Church in history, we see much that is unworthy and that seems to contradict the ideal-izing claims made for it, we recognize that, if it is an earthen vessel, it contains and exists for and by a Treasure, and that the actual, which is yet incomplete and growing, must be viewed in the light of this ideal which is at once its inspiration and the goal of its journey through time.

II

The well-known notes of the Church tell how she is One, Holy, Catholic, Apostolic.

(*a*) She is *One*, and in spite of divisions knows herself as one because her Head is one and the Spirit indwelling her is one. And as there is but one Christ and one Spirit, she can never rest in the thought of herself as anything else than one. She is one in tendency, in sin, in endeavour, in expectation. Are we to feel surprise if a mere nineteen hundred years have not brought into harmony the unruly wills and affections which in secular affairs we see contending together between the nations and between the individuals who compose the nations?

We are only beginning to-day to appreciate the size and com-plexity and the deep-lying divisions of the human material out of which mankind is built, and it is only as we feel the con-fusion of that human chaos that we become aware of the vast-ness and splendour and withal the difficulty of the task that lies before the Church of making Christian believers, let alone the human race, one in Christ. The One Christ has made His Church one. In spite of the obscuring of that unity in the empirical "churches", the common belief in the Person of the one Christ is forcing believers in Him to seek to actualize the unity which belongs to the Church by virtue of its one Head, in Whom it is God's purpose to gather all things together in one.

(b) The Church is *Holy*. She is holy because Christ is holy; holy, not because she can claim to have arrived at any perfection of holiness, but because the head of the Church has consecrated her to holiness. The Church is the redeemed society, the fellow-ship of those who are being schooled in holiness. Called to be holy, with the means of grace freely offered to them, they respond and are led on in the way of holiness. That there should be some, or many, who fail to respond through ignorance or wilful-ness, is neither a condemnation of the Society which seeks their good nor a justification for departing from it on the part of those who shrink from contact with others who seem to be living below the strictest standard.

Whatever the defilement of human sin, even in the regenerate, it is beyond doubt that holiness is the aim, to the pursuit of which the Church is dedicated, and that in Christ the Church is indefectibly committed to holiness as it is to the belief in the forgiveness of sins.

At the worst of times, there has always been a faithful remnant. Whatever may be said by way of detraction, the Church forms a standing conscience to the world, which knows well enough that the sins of Christians do not truly represent the moral standard of the Church but are grossly inconsistent with it. For even when the leaders of the Church have failed signally, the *sensus communis* of the rank and file has carried on the sacred tradition.

Secular society is little conscious of its obligation, but such sense of truth and justice and respect for the individual as it possesses is drawn from, or at least is firmly supported by, the Christian Church, that treasury of the mind and principles of Christ.

(c) The Church is *Catholic*, or *Universal*. Unlike the Jewish Ecclesia, which was exclusive as being confined to the covenant-people, the Christian Ecclesia is universal in its range, and is for all God's children whatever their race or colour or tongue. As the visible symbol of the largeness of God's purposes for mankind and the instrument for effecting them, it is its duty to go into all the world, to preach the whole Gospel to every creature.

The subject of its teaching is the revealed truth to which the New Testament, as heir of the Old Testament, the ancient fathers, the great Councils and the consent of the Church from age to age bear witness. Its business is not to declare new truths, but faithfully to hand on the deposit which had been accepted always, everywhere and by all.

At the same time, the Church is Catholic, because all truth everywhere is of God, and nothing that is a revelation of the ways and mind of God can be outside its scope.

Christian thinkers and students and teachers can ill afford to neglect the assured results of scientific investigation, of intellectual enquiry or critical research. Truth is of God, and the Church of Christ Who is the Truth must not be unduly slow in coming face to face with the questionings or the affirmations which proceed from the minds of honest seekers after truth.

The Church is placed in the world to speak with authority concerning the revealed Truth which it possesses by age-long inheritance; but its authority will commend itself the better to an enquiring age if it is known that it honestly takes account of, and checks its position and utterances by the light that comes pouring in from every quarter of God's world.

(d) The Church is *Apostolic*. Our Lord said to the assembled company on the night of His Resurrection, " As my Father hath sent me, even so send I you." He gives a mission to His Church even as He had received His mission from God.

The Church exists by divine authority, and authority in the Church was committed to the Apostles who were divinely designated as its organs to exercise in it a permanent stewardship of grace and truth. Thus, not only was a Society established but it received the beginnings of a structure. The Church grew up round its Apostolic Ministry. There is a "given-ness" both in its faith and in its form. In the Church, whether in regard to the given-ness of its faith or of its ministry, we see an illustration not of evolution upwards but of devolution downwards. Its organization was of necessity loose and flexible to begin with, its general ministry passing into the local ministry, but involved in it there lay certain governing elements of authority and continuity necessary for the preservation of its identity. And thus the Church was no self-appointed or self-governing democracy. It acknowledged an abiding and directing constraint upon its freedom exercised by the Apostolic stewards whom Christ in the beginning had set over His earthly household. This authoritative constraint manifests itself down the ages most noticeably in two connections, viz., in the Faith delivered through the Apostles, and in the historic ministry set within it from Apostolic days, "the very nerve and sinew of ecclesiastical unity and communion" (John Bramhall), as the organ for the performance of the corporate actions of the society.

III

The most important duties laid upon this visible Church are three in number—(a) that of witnessing to the revealed Truth of God in Christ, (b) that of the worship of God, and (c) that of teaching men to live as children of the Heavenly Father.

Witness to the Truth. God who in many parts and in many fashions spoke in past days to the Fathers through the prophets, spoke in these last days in a Son. Christianity is Christ, or rather the Godhead as revealed in and through the Person of Christ. The progressive revelation of God through the prophets of the Old Testament is followed and completed by the self-revelation of the Father through the Incarnate Word. And it is to declare God in Christ, and to lead mankind to see the world of men and things in the light of that disclosure that the Church was sent on its way.

The knowledge of the Truth is intended to lead on to *Worship.* Man's highest duty and privilege is, with reverence and godly fear, to acknowledge and bow before and give glory to his Creator, his Father, all holy, all sovereign and all pitying.

The Church has to live in the world as leader and teacher of God's creatures in their adoring wonder at the majesty and perfection and saving grace of God, and in their voluntary submission to, and execution of His will.

Christ, the High Priest of mankind in the heavenly Temple, presents before God His unceasing Self-oblation and intercession, and with Him the Church which is His Body is to be taught to join, as it yields itself to God with the heart-homage of instructed praise and devout thanksgiving.

The Church's duty in the world is also to teach men *how to live*. It is the home and channel of grace through the indwelling Spirit of Christ. It is the supreme witness to love, the love of Christ which binds Him to His spouse the Church and the Church to Him; to the love of its members for one another whereby in the fellowship and peace of the Holy Ghost they live the corporate life of mutual service and loyalty; and to the Christian ethic based on the teaching given by Christ and His Apostles and on the personal example bequeathed by Christ Himself. The visible Church as it discharges these duties exercises an influence on a civilization, often hostile and commonly indifferent, whether for judgment or inspiration, both salutary and vivifying.

Nevertheless the Great Church is not a temporal power. It must not stand in any formal way over against the State. It has no country, no Courts of Justice, no General Headquarters, no Diplomatic Corps, nor does it commit itself to treaties or concordats. The meeting of a General Council is the rarest of events. As a Corporation as much spiritual as temporal it is by nature too elusive for the conduct of secular negotiations, but it must operate on the world indirectly through its members.

Just as the pressure of the atmosphere is silent and imperceptible and yet real and universal, so the visible Church exercises its pressure and its moral authority through its members who are bound to it by bonds invisible as well as visible, who, if they use the Grace given to them, can diffuse the influence of their Society at all points of their contact with the citizens of the secular State. It is in this way that, though the Church must always be more or less at cross-purposes with the world, the standard of public opinion and morals can be upheld and raised, by the determined upward thrust of that *sensus communis* which the Church, in the exercise of its prophetic office, quickens and shapes and builds in the consciousness of its children.

.   .   .   .

The Great Church, for all its supramundane relations, is an institution in this world and discernible as such. The tragedy of our divisions is precisely that we are not agreed about the necessary "marks" by which "the Church" is discerned. Those who belong to the Anglican communion believe themselves to have inherited, by God's mercy and not of their own deserving, the marks of an essential catholicity. However much their expression may to-day have been obscured and need reform, these essentials must be part of any fully Catholic Church.

Essential Catholicism, in its view, involves a background of four fundamental and indispensable elements, viz.: (1) Holy Scripture as the final criterion by which all beliefs claimed as necessarily to be confessed for salvation are to be tested; (2) the full faith of the Apostles' Creed and the Nicene Creed; (3) the unfailing use of the two great Sacraments of the Gospel as ordained by Christ, and (4) the Apostolic Ministry of Bishops, Priests and Deacons, transmitted by those having authority to transmit.

The Book of Common Prayer presents the body of practice accompanying and interpreting for the Church of England these four traditional elements in the Catholic position. But just as in the Anglican system many variations of that book have taken shape in the sister and daughter churches of the Anglican Communion, so in the branches of the Great Church an infinite variety of rite is compatible with loyalty to the Catholic norm, which from early days has admitted without uneasiness the practical necessity in a world-wide fellowship of " *Salvo jure communionis diversa sentire* ", or again of " in things essential, unity; in things doubtful, liberty; in all things, charity ".

In conclusion, a Church claiming to be Catholic must not be content with a self-regarding enjoyment of its Faith. Not merely does it possess the Faith, but the Faith possesses it. And the Faith, by its Apostolic nature, drives it to look outwards and to seek fellowship with other bodies of Christians. The establishment or restoration of communion with separated bodies of Christians must be one of its most serious concerns. For there should be no schism in the Body of Christ. And yet schism is one of the most palpable and painful facts of Christian history. The Great Church's witness to the world, to say nothing of its own growth in holiness, is hampered to an incalculable extent by the divisions prevailing among the baptized members of Christ's Church.

Yet no yearnings after a closer fellowship can justify the

E

entering into communion with a society which has lost, and shows no desire to recover, its hold upon any one of those few but vital institutions specified above which are the visible pledges of continuity with the undivided Church.

Thus the Great Church to-day is conscious of a tragic tension between necessities seemingly irreconcilable. But the Church is not a voluntary association which can make its own terms. It is a trustee with an unbroken succession of the deposit once for all delivered, and its trust determines coercively for its member-churches how each, as a pillar and buttress of the truth, is to shape its invitations and its responses. Thus, paradoxically enough, many Anglicans who in principle are ardently desirous for fellowship between their own and other communions, are compelled to resist any proposals for union which either deny the sufficiency or threaten the integrity of the Church's inherited faith or order.

Divisions between separated bodies of Christians which recognize in one another the workings of the one Spirit, need not forbid mutual respect, or endeavours after a better understanding or co-operation in social reform, nor need they any longer attract the world's attention and contempt by manifestations of controversial acerbity. On the other hand, comprehension at the cost of unlawful compromise would be no better than a bridge which broke in the middle.

5

THE CHURCH—THE LIVING CONGREGATION[1]
OF THE LIVING LORD JESUS CHRIST

by Karl Barth

THE title of this paper constitutes a *definition* of the idea, "Church". It is a positive description of what the Church *is*. Negatively, however, it goes further, for it tacitly eliminates all that may bear the name of "Church" but is not so in reality: a merely nominal church, an ecclesiastical shell from which the life has fled.

The definition describes the Church as a *congregation*, a subject, which is confronted by, and controlled by another primary subject: *Jesus Christ* as absolute Lord (Creator, Preserver, Owner, Governor); the Church (as "congregation") is only a *living* Church in so far as it is filled with the life of this primary subject, and only if its life is based on this foundation is it a *real* Church.

What the Church is: the congregation *is*, or *exists*, where, and in so far as it dares to live by the act of its living Lord.

The danger menacing the Church: the congregation fails to *exist* when, and in so far as the foundations of its life are shaken by its own sins and errors.

The renewal of the Church: the congregation is preserved and is saved by the ever-new acts of its Lord. The meaning of its life and its calling consists in being continually open to Him, ready to perceive these "signs of His appearing".

I WHAT THE CHURCH IS

The period in which the congregation is living is that of *the End*, that is, the period containing the particular, final History between God and man, which began with the Resurrection of Jesus Christ from the dead, and will reach its close and its con-

[1] German: *Gemeinde*. In this paper Barth uses the word "Gemeinde" to denote the *worshipping community*, meeting regularly in a given place, entirely dependent on the continually new activity of the Lord Jesus Christ. (Translator.)

summation in the open manifestation of the reconciliation between God and the whole of creation, already effected in Him.

In this final period the congregation is the *event*[2] which consists in gathering together (congregatio) those men and women (fidelium) whom the living Lord Jesus Christ chooses and calls to be witnesses to the victory He has already won, and heralds of its future universal manifestation.

The congregation is the result of a process by which certain people are differentiated from others, and are drawn into fellowship with one another by Jesus Christ, through a common experience of the Divine Mercy, which is also Judgment, and of the Divine Judgment which is also Mercy, a common experience of gratitude towards God, and a common desire to serve their neighbours, which leads them to the discovery that *together*, they have a mission to the world outside.

The congregation is that event in which the absolute sovereignty of Jesus Christ—its Lord, and also the Lord of the world—finds its proper answer and response in the perfect freedom of obedience of those who have been called, called out, and called together by Him, and summoned to gratitude and to service.

The congregation is that event in which these men—for whom the work of Jesus Christ as the Reconciler of the world with God has become a revealed Word, the Word of Truth, which lays its obligation upon them—unite together over against the world; yet only in order that they may identify themselves with the need and the hope of the world.

The congregation is the event in which the witness of apostles and prophets to Jesus Christ, deposited in Scripture, as such, becomes present, effective and fruitful; and its authority visible and intelligible in a continual process of research, exposition and preaching.

The congregation is the event in which the communion of the Holy Ghost also establishes, with divine power, a human fellowship, derived from the acceptance of the Word of Jesus Christ in and through the witness of the Bible, heard and perceived in common; this produces a concord of faith and creed, of love and its works, of hope and its confidence, made available for all mankind.

[2] German: *Ereignis*. The writer means that the Church is not constituted once for all, but that it is continually being re-created by renewed divine activity. No single English word can express this idea, which lies behind the word "event" as used in this paper. (Translator.)

The congregation is the event in which the Sacraments are powerful as the one reality by which men live: Baptism, which incorporates human beings into this special relation to Jesus Christ, and the Lord's Supper, which keeps them in this state of grace, that is, of "belonging to Him", and enables them to fulfil their mission to others.

The congregation is the event in which the divine mission of Jesus Christ is represented and attested: through the preaching of His Word, through the invitation to believe on Him, and also through the manifestation of the temporal, political and social significance of the salvation that has appeared in Him in the midst of the "non-Christian" world (for which nevertheless He died and rose again).

The explanation of the idea of the "Church" by means of the idea of the "congregation" is significant and useful only if "congregation" is explicitly understood as a "living congregation"; that is, as a congregation as described in the preceding paragraphs, which consists in the *event* by which it is *gathered* together: that is, the congregation as the decisive element in this final phase in the story of God's relations with man. It is precisely this history which, as such, constitutes the Church; that is "what the Church *is*".

II THE DANGER MENACING THE CHURCH

The life of the Church is both secured and endangered: its security comes from above; its danger from below.

Its life is secured (*perpetuo mansura est*) by the indissoluble life of its Head, the Lord Jesus Christ, risen from the dead: through the final validity of His work accomplished once for all; through the power of His Word and His Spirit; through the inexhaustible nature of the witness of apostles and prophets to Him; through the validity of the signs instituted by Him in Baptism and the Lord's Supper; and through the unceasing fidelity with which He watches over His congregation.

The life of the Church is *endangered* (the Church can and does fall into temptation), for the following reasons: because the life of Christ's congregation is "creaturely" in character; because it cannot be absolutely protected against the possibility of falling into unbelief or error, into lovelessness and doubt, that is, against the possibility of dissolution and of death; but it can be given a *de facto* protection only, which consists in the occurrence of that "event" in which the activity of Jesus Christ is stronger than all human sin.

One form of this danger which threatens the Church, through human error, can be seen when the Bible, dogma, the catechism, church order, the liturgy, preaching, and sacrament, instead of being documents and instruments within the congregation become mere museum pieces; when the Kingdom of God that has "come upon" men in Jesus Christ becomes a vague realm of venerable truths and exalted moral principles; when the free grace of God's Word and Spirit becomes the routine of a religious and moral code. If in such conditions the congregation affirms what it believes, it does so without joy, because it has no sense of urgent need, no impulse to ask, and seek, and knock, no sense of dissatisfaction; and therefore also no impulse to share with others. Such a congregation—in spite of all its assertions to the contrary—is at heart unsure of itself, uncertain in its faith; hence it can only "keep up appearances" before the world; its reality and its impressiveness are hollow.

Another form of this danger which threatens the Church through human error, appears when the attention and loyalty of the congregation is divided between what it ought to do for the world, in the service of its Lord, and according to His teaching, and what it feels bound to do from all sorts of other considerations—for "the need of the moment", for society at large, for political and economic realities, for the tendencies of the dominant culture with its own philosophy of life and its own ethical tradition, or even for the specific traditions of its own church life and order. When this situation arises, the congregation lives and preaches a so-called "Christianity", which is actually a mixture of elements in which that which is alien to real Christianity always tries to get the upper hand.

Another form of this danger to the Church through human error appears when the congregation absolutely forgets its peculiar endowment and its mission, and devotes itself to the concerns and wishes, the convictions and endeavours of the "Christian" people who constitute its membership, concerns which are foreign, and perhaps even directly opposed to, its relation to Jesus Christ. Then faith in the Gospel degenerates into religiosity, love becomes devotion to certain "ideals", hope becomes confidence in all kinds of social and individual progress.

The Bible is interpreted by alien criteria, and quietly ceases to be read or used. It is then only a question of time before the Creed loses all meaning, public worship ceases, evangelism disappears, and the "Church" of this kind has no vital message for the world; it is dumb and silent. The Church has now itself become the world, a "religious" world, with a prophetic ministry so weak and feeble that the world can well afford to ignore it altogether.

The common element in all forms of this danger to the Church consists in the fact that the history, the movement, the action begun by the first subject, by Jesus Christ, is not continued in the other subject, in His congregation, but suffers from arrested development. The vital current passing and repassing between the Lord and His congregation is blocked by man's sin. The life of the congregation ceases to be "event"; the congregation ceases to be a *living* congregation. But this means that the Church has ceased to exist.

In itself, and as such, the Church could long since, and everywhere, have succumbed to this danger. She could long since have passed away and perished as the result of her own sin. The fact that her disease only affects certain spheres of her life, and does not infect everything, is due to the sovereignty, the faithfulness, and the patience of her Lord. Even then, the Church must be on her guard against this disease, which might be fatal. She must always bear in mind that spiritual carelessness may lead to the final tragedy when, as a congregation, her Lord may say unto her: "Thou hast a name that thou livest, and art dead."

The place of the church that is no longer a church is not replaced by a vacuum. Instead we have the phenomenon of the nominal church, or the church which is merely an ecclesiastical shell: the ecclesiastical *quid pro quo*, endowed with all the qualities (but deprived of all their content) of the really living congregation. In this situation two things may happen: the congregation that has long been dead may be on good terms with society and the State, because it constitutes no threat to the world around it; or—the fact that it is so feeble and has so little influence on the world may bring external judgment upon it. So the phenomenon of the congregation which is dead, and yet still maintains its external existence, must always be regarded from a twofold point of view: on the one hand, as a sign of the extreme gravity of the danger hanging over it, and, on the other hand, as a sign of the patience of God, Who can raise men to new life, even from the grave.

The visible sign of the danger which menaces the Church is the loss of her unity. Her unity stands and falls with that " event " which is the " gathering " of the congregation by the Word and the Spirit of her living Lord, Jesus Christ. If this divine activity is even partially checked, the congregation itself disintegrates, and congregations fall apart. For a living and a dead congregation cannot be a single congregation; there can be neither friendship nor peace between living and dead congregations. Even the necessary service of the living congregation to one that is dead must retain the form of open contradiction until unity in Jesus Christ has once more become an " event ", until the dead congregation has once more been quickened into life. Even then the living congregation finds itself plunged into all kinds of difficult and painful questions about the severity and the clemency the situation requires (e.g. the problem of the relation between the Law and the Gospel in the " Church Struggle " and in theological controversy!).

III THE RENEWAL OF THE CHURCH

The life of the Church is preserved, and saved in one way alone: by the renewal of her life as an " event ", and thus by the renewal of her " gathering " as a congregation. A church that is not thus engaged in a reformation corresponding to the way in which she was originally " formed ", has already fallen into the abyss of non-existence, or, in other words, she has fallen into the hopeless condition of a nominal church, or an empty ecclesiastical shell.

The renewal of the living congregation, which also constitutes her unification, is the work of her living Lord: the new light and the new power of His Word, according to the testimony of the Bible, the new outpouring of His Spirit, and His new Presence in preaching and in worship, in Baptism and the Lord's Supper. No danger can touch Him. He alone, in the power of His endless life, is so triumphantly adequate to deal with the sins and errors of the life of the Christian Church that He can both preserve and save it. He alone is the hope of the Church.

But the congregation must see to it that her church-order

makes room for that "event" which constitutes her renewal by the new acts of her Lord. The task and the significance of church-order consists in so uniting the congregation on the human level that it is rendered as free as possible for all that the Lord Himself can, and will do in her.

The Church is neither the invisible fellowship, nor the visible community, of all those who believe in Christ; nor is it a monarchical, aristocratic, or democratic form of the latter. The Church is the "event" in which two or three are gathered together in the name of Jesus Christ, i.e. in the power of His calling and commission. Church order is concerned exclusively with this event, with the living congregation itself.

The primary, normal, and visible form of this event is the *local congregation*, meeting in a "parish" or "district" with clearly defined boundaries. Such a local congregation is constituted by the possibility and the actuality of regular public worship, i.e. common worship at which the Atonement made by Jesus is proclaimed, as the ground of our hope. The Church lives (she *is*) in this visible, concrete, transaction (prayer, confession of faith, Baptism, Lord's Supper, the proclamation and reception of the Gospel), and in its presuppositions (theology, training of the young), and its consequences (brotherly discipline, pastoral care and other oversight). The Church lives (she actually *is*) in the form of a local congregation, which is the basis of all other forms of her life.

The government that guarantees the unity of the living congregation is the concern of her living Lord alone, and of His Word attested by the Scriptures. Apart from Him there is no ecclesiastical office (*officium*). There can only be the *service* (*Diakonia, ministerium*) of the whole congregation, divided and organized in relation to all that worship requires, both in that which it presupposes, and that to which it leads. For the fulfilment of this service all the members of the congregation are responsible together, as a whole, in which all share; in this service, for practical reasons some may have to take precedence of others, but in principle there are no "higher" or "lower" forms of service. Such service can be shared among the members only on the basis of a recognition of the different gifts bestowed by the one Holy Spirit, Who is promised to all.

The question about church order arises again when we turn to the relation of different local congregations to each other.

Since each of them, in its immediate relation to the one Lord, is in the fullest sense of the word a Church, i.e. a congregation, they can only mutually acknowledge each other, stand by each other in their life as congregations, advise, help, and to this extent, guide one another. But such " guidance ", or " direction ", is not domination or authority, but service. Neither individual dignitaries nor a clerical body can be considered the organ for this special service; the only organ for such " guidance " is that constituted by a special congregation, viz. a *synodical congregation* (whether regional, national—or ecumenical?) which is made up *ad hoc* of certain members from other congregations, sharing in the same life, and celebrating public worship in the same way.

The task of the synod or " synodal congregation " consists in securing, as far as is humanly possible, the co-ordination and solidarity, the catholic and " ecumenical " character of the life of those individual congregations associated with it. To do this it will set up and exercise a spiritual law in spiritual authority. It will be quite as much concerned about a forward policy as about the need to preserve a good tradition. In all this it will be simply one free congregation among others, standing alongside of, and yet representing them all. But in the fulfilment of its special task, and indeed of the very purpose of its existence, as a true mother-congregation it will see to it that in the special matters with which it is concerned the churches associated with it will receive counsel and challenge to action, advice and rebuke, but above all, evangelical encouragement. " Church government " as such, however, will not be its concern, but must remain in the hands of Him Who is Lord of all His many congregations.

There are, however, some cross-relations between individual local congregations, and other forms and organs of their unity. These are the *free associations for service* in the cause of charity, education, missions at home and abroad; further, within the bounds set by the one gift and calling that makes the Church the Church, there may also be associations for the guidance of Christian thought and policy. Such bodies should regard themselves quite seriously—and not only *de facto* but also *de iure*— as worshipping congregations, and should behave accordingly. In common with the local congregations and their associated synods, they also live by the grace given to the one Church, and in fulfilling their service to the one Church, they too are churches in the full sense of the word.

Church order, like the Church itself, is not an end in itself. It is man's attempt so to serve God's Word in obedience to it, that, in face of the danger menacing the Church, the wisest, boldest and most effective steps are taken to ensure that the immediate meeting and communion of the living Lord Jesus Christ with His congregation shall take place anew. No human effort can ensure this divine encounter. But man *can* clear the obstacles out of the way; and *this* is the purpose of church order.

The objection to the *papal* church order, and, in lesser degree, also to the *episcopal, consistorial,* and *presbyterian-synodal* church order, is that these systems obstruct the free access of God's Word to the actual congregation, and that they come between the congregation and the Word. All these systems of church order are due, more or less, to a quite unnecessary fear of arbitrary human action on the part of those who are chosen and called to be members of the living congregation of Jesus Christ, coupled with a scandalous lack of concern about the arbitrary behaviour of certain officials, chosen and appointed by men, to wield authority within, and over, the Church. Where the renewal of the Church is concerned, fear of the liberty of the Lord Jesus Christ, or fear of the liberty of His congregation is no help at all. Further, an indirect criticism of these systems of church order arises out of the contemporary situation: churches built on these principles are quite unable to show, as they ought, any example in their own Church life to the peoples of the world, who are everywhere in such need of political renewal.

Not even the *Congregationalist* church order is above criticism. Its representatives have not yet been able to offer a satisfactory answer to the problem of the unity of the Church and of the churches. This paper is not a plea for the uncritical adoption of this particular system. But the principle of Congregationalism—the free congregation of the free Word of God—is sound enough. At any rate, certain elements of Congregationalism are absolutely indispensable for other proposals for church order if these are not to lead to disorder, but to create real order. From this standpoint too the ecumenical unity of the Church can be seen more freely than anywhere else. It is obvious that the last remnants of sovereign authority in the idea of a *corpus christianum* are disappearing; this suggests that we should now look in this other (Congregationalist) direction. Indirectly, this argument receives further confirmation in the reflection that a Church formed on the basis of these principles would be an event of exemplary importance in the political world of the present day.

II

THE SHAME AND GLORY OF THE CHURCH

———

However diverse our interpretations of the nature of the Church, the whole body of Christians knows certain things quite clearly in experience. We all know the shame of finding the life of our churches permeated by the disorder of the world. The first of the essays in this section deals with the nature and the depth of that disorder.

We all know, too, with gratitude, how the glory of God can be made manifest in the witness of the Church. The second and third essays speak out of the heart of recent experience of that God-given victory. Whilst Bishop Fjellbu writes, for the sake of concreteness, only from the background of Norway, he testifies to an experience equally known to the Church in many other European countries and in parts of Asia. Dr. Schlink and Dr. von Thadden speak for the Church upon whom fell the first and the hardest part of the struggle to manifest God's glory amidst man's disorder.

1

THE DISORDER OF MAN IN THE
CHURCH OF GOD

by H. Richard Niebuhr

I

A T the outset of our effort to measure and understand the
disorder of man in the Church of God we shall do well to
remind ourselves of some general guiding principles.

First: we can rightly think and speak of this disorder only in
the way of Christian repentance. There are many false and
essentially disorderly ways of diagnosing what is wrong with the
Church. Outsiders, for instance, may criticize it for failing to
measure up to one of the various standards they employ. As
nationalists or communists, as political liberals or political con-
servatives, as humanists, naturalists or idealists, they bring their
particular notions of good and evil to bear on the Church and
call on it to change its ways. Within the Church also there are
ways of diagnosing and criticizing disorder which are not
characterized by the spirit of repentance. Fault-finding directed
towards other individuals or groups in the Church is one of
these, for such fault-finding is as distinct from repentance as it
is from brotherly admonition. Again, emotional shame, remorse
and self-accusation in the Church do not always manifest "godly
sorrow" working repentance, but may exhibit the "sorrow of
the world" working death (2 Cor. vii, 9-11). Repentance distinguishes itself from such an attitude in two ways. On the one
hand it is an active turning away from sin rather than a morbid
feeling. On the other hand it is hopeful, looking towards the
healing of diseases, while remorse and shame, in so far as they
remain worldly, are hopeless. Finally, there is a sort of self-
criticism in the Church, which is not repentance in the Christian
sense, because it is the counterpart of faith in the self rather
than of faith in God. When we practise it we do so as those
who believe that by means of one more effort to correct ourselves
we shall overcome our disorder. In such repentance our chief
disorder—our self-will, our determination to direct ourselves,

our faith in ourselves—remains hidden from us. Christian repentance is the counterpart of Christian faith. As faith is the
turning towards God in trust and reliance on Him, so repentance
is the turning away from the self and its idols as the beings in
which we have confidence and from which we expect our salvation. It is only in the spirit of such repentance and such faith
that we can be bold enough in the Church to attempt to understand our sin.

Secondly: the disorder to which our attention is called in
repentance is not so much the disorder *of* the Church as disorder
in the Church. In certain ecumenical meetings held in the past
representatives of some sections of the Church have objected to
statements that the Church needs to repent, or that it is sinful.
This objection has a true basis, recognizable by all of us who
confess our belief in the Church as an integral part of our statement of faith in the Triune God. The Church as the community
and Body of Christ, as the holy and whole people of God, as the
City of God in heaven and on earth, is the mediator of grace and
not of sin, of order and not of disorder. Disorder resides in ourselves and not in it. Yet disorder is in ourselves not as individuals
only but also as organized parts of the Church, as vocational,
national, ethnic and historical organs of its body. We are never
merely individual church members but always also members of
one of the special groups which constitute the whole community.
It is in these groups as well as in our privacy that we hear the
call to repentance. To-day we learn of our disorder not only as
national or denominational parts of the Church, but also as the
part of the Church located in the twentieth century.

Thirdly: we do well to remember that our disorder is not so
much a state of affairs as an action of disordering, just as, on the
other hand, order in the Church is not a static arrangement of
its parts but the constant action of ordering by its Head. Individuals called to repentance by the Gospel sometimes seek to
evade that call by reflecting that their sin is a state of miserable
existence to which they have been reduced by earlier actions of
their own or by the actions of their fathers. They ignore the fact
that each repetition on their part of a disorderly action of the
past involves a new consent of their wills, and that each repetition introduces fresh disorder into their lives. They also forget
that they may be acting sinfully when they repeat in a present
moment what was at one time right action but is no longer

fitting, as when the mature man behaves in a way that was required of the child. In similar fashion organized members of the Church are tempted to place responsibility for present disorder on some action of their fathers. So sectarians tend to blame present church-disorganization on the Constantinian settlement, calling that the fall of Christianity, while Protestants may make the rise of the Papacy, and Roman Catholics the Reformation, the source of the Church's disorder. The call to repentance meets us in the Church not as those who are disordered by past actions, but as those who are disordering by present actions, whether these be repetitions of actions which were sinful in the past and are now sinful, or repetitions of actions which were done sincerely and in obedience to God by our fathers, but which we can only repeat in disobedience to Him.

Our fourth and final preliminary reflection is that man's disorder in the Church of God is a relative thing. As it is certain that we cannot in repentance know our sin without at the same time knowing in faith God's grace, so also it is certain that our disordering action in the Church is nothing absolute or independent, but is dependent on the presence of God's fundamental action of ordering. In the same vision in which we see the abundance of our sin we see the abundance of God's grace. If all were disorder there would be no Church at all. Where there is disease in the physical body, that is, disorder, there must also be health, that is, some right order; otherwise there would be no body at all which could live, even in diseased condition, and as fighting against its disease. This is the condition which we discern in the Church. Hence our repentance does not turn to despair, for it is the counterpart of that faith which knows the present action of divine grace. On the other hand our faith does not lead us into the temptation to become complacent and to accept our sin as inevitable or as not requiring repentance, for it is faith in the Saviour who rouses us out of our despair and our complacency with the question, "Wilt thou be made whole?"

II

When in such repentant faith and believing repentance we examine ourselves in the Church of God we become aware that there is no area of our existence in which sin does not seem to prevail. We are almost baffled by its pervasive, complex and radical nature. Yet we must seek to understand it. In this effort we may be assisted if we use the Scriptural analogy and regard the Church as the Body of Christ, made up of many members or organs. We note, then, that the disorder of man manifests itself in God's Church in at least four spheres: within the organs themselves, in the relations of the organs to each other, in the relations of the organs to the world, and, finally, in their relations to the Head. What in this complex confusion of disorder is symptom, what source or cause, we do not now inquire as we seek to know something of the extent of our distress.

We may regard the groups called denominations, national churches, vocational orders such as the clergy, local congregations and other associations of Christians, as organs of the body. What sorts of disorder are present in them? What sins abound in the intricate inter-relations of individual Christians to one another and to the organic unit? A factionalism like that described in 1 Corinthians doubtless appears in some, perhaps all, the organs. A loveless discipline which simply casts out offenders against the common rule marks the conduct of others. But perhaps the disorder of which we are most aware in many parts of the Church is the sin which is the opposite of both these former ones: loveless lack of discipline. We tend to purchase our unity at the price of principle and our peace with one another at the cost of genuine mutual service. This situation is connected with the character of the membership of our groups.

As in the days of Augustine "there are many reprobate mingled with the good and both are gathered together by the gospel as in a drag-net". Yet we are forced to admit that the drag-net in our case has often been some other agency than the Gospel. Whether we have sought to expand our organizations in the Church through the direct political measures which created state churches, or have as free churches entered into competition for popular support with other Christian organizations and also with secular institutions, in any case, we have managed to bring into our churches many who have made no personal commitment to the Lord and His cause. When we contemplate what happened to the churches of Germany in their hour of sifting and winnowing, there are not many of us in other countries or in other Christian groups who can sincerely say that

F

their membership contains a smaller proportion of the half-hearted, the luke-warm, of potential or actual deniers and traitors. It would doubtless be disorderly on our part to seek to anticipate the ordering action of the Lord of the Church Who sifts the wheat from the chaff on the threshing-floors of history, yet this does not excuse our more present disobedience both in continuing to gather into the Church those whom we do not call by the Gospel, and in withholding from those who have been so gathered adequate instruction and training in the exercise of genuine Christian vocation.

The first of these disordering actions brings into our churches many folk for whom "religion" is a part of a respectable life, or who pick and choose among the many "values" which the Church offers those which appeal to them. When, for the sake of meeting the wishes of such members, we withhold the challenge of the Gospel and turn it into an easy doctrine which demands no hard decisions, no continued self-denial in political and economic as in private matters, no surrender of the whole self to Christ, then we are guilty of the second part of this disorder. What in this realm is sincere adaptation to the needs of people, what self-deception, what is nominal and what is genuine Christianity, none of us can decide for others. Yet that there is much disorder here is patent, and that corporate as well as individual decisions about the conditions and requirements of church membership must be made seems also clear.

III

We have been made most acutely aware in our time of a second group of disorganizing actions in the Church, namely those which set the parts of the Church, the organic members of the body of Christ, at variance with each other and so disturb, distract and inhibit the functioning of the whole body. These disorganizing actions of ours appear in various forms. Sometimes they are actions of self-isolation in which as local congregations, or as national and ethnic churches or as confessional groups we say in effect to other members of the Body of Christ, "We have no need of you." Again they are actions of conflict in which we contend against other parts of the body as though they were alien and inimical to the body itself. While this disorder seems particularly characteristic of the relations of the Protestant and

Roman communities in the Church of Christ, it also appears in inter-Protestant and in Protestant-Orthodox relations. Again there are the disorganizing actions of those who seek special honour or prestige, as when a community of the clergy claim, or permit themselves to receive, a position in the Church which separates them from the lay orders. These various disorganizing actions may have a touch of imperialism in them, as when some one part of the Church undertakes to extend its rule over other parts, as though its own relations to the Head were more direct than that of the rest.

If the manifestations of disorder in these relations are manifold its roots seem to be manifold also. One apparent source is the social interplay in which action calls forth response in kind. As in the political sphere nationalism in one country calls forth nationalism in its neighbours, so, in the Church, self-sufficient denominationalism in one part tempts others to take the same attitude. Attack invites counter-attack so that anti-Romanism and anti-Protestantism, anti-liberalism and anti-orthodoxy flourish together. A second and more prevalent source of disorder lies in the confusion of a part with the whole. Thus a part of the Church regards itself as the whole or as representative of the whole, or it confuses the statement of what is most evidently true for it with the whole truth of the Gospel, or, again, it believes that the rule which it must follow in the performance of its function is the rule which the whole Church and all its other parts ought to follow. It may even believe that its particular function is the one function which the whole Church ought to carry out. Christendom is full of these confusions and so multiplicity of order is converted into disorder by the absolutizing of every relative, ordered pattern of action. The graciousness which marks some of the relations of distinct geographical, historical and vocational organs or groups in the Church is accompanied by much ingratitude to and for each other. We accept the correction, limitation and complementation of one by the other unwillingly and, rather than remain in the community of forgiveness and truly common faith, we separate from each other by withdrawal or excommunication.

These disorders among the organs of the Church appear most evidently in their external organization and even more in their lack of ecumenical order. They are, however, equally present and perhaps more destructive in the spiritual relations, as when in their prayers, their proclamation of the Gospel and their theological deliberation parts of the Church are either unmindful of one another or mind only those things in each other which invite correction. In this situation we impoverish ourselves as well as others, and as a result of our poverty have less and less to give to a world in need.

A multiplicity of special groups in the Church, serving men for God's sake in many diverse places and situations and cultures and performing many special functions, may be a sign of obedience to one Master and hence of order rather than of disorder. The presence in these congregations, denominations, and associations of many different special types of organization may also be indicative of such obedience. What is disorderly is isolation, contempt for each other, the pretension to special honour, the claim of the part to be the whole, the refusal to live in active inter-dependence, the effort to reign over others.

IV

The third sphere in which repentance discovers our human sin in the Church of God is in our relation as organized parts of the Church to the world outside the Church. Faith knows what action in this sphere is commanded by the Lord of the Church. Positively, our action is orderly when, following that command, we go into the world to make disciples of all nations, to baptize them and to teach them all that has been commanded to the Church. Negatively, it is ordered action when it is unspotted by the corruption and love of the world (Romans xii, 2; James i, 27; 1 John ii, 15). In the light of that double order we discern the confusion which has entered into our church-world relations. On the other hand, going into the world we become disciples of the world so that we import into the Church the corruptions of the world. Then in reaction to our secularism we are tempted to withdraw from the world and to seek holiness in isolation from it. Or, again, our ordered action in making disciples of Jesus Christ becomes the disordered action of those who seek to make converts to themselves rather than to Him and to teach such converts to observe not what our Lord has commanded us to do, but what we command them to do. Thus in our relations to the world we are tempted and often fall into the sins of secularism, of sectarianism, and of proselytism, using that last term to designate the sin which Jesus chastised when He said, "Woe to you, scribes and Pharisees, hypocrites! for you traverse sea and land to make a single proselyte, and when he becomes a proselyte, you make him twice as much a child of hell as yourselves."

The disorder of secularism is perhaps nowhere more apparent in our contemporary Church than in the extent to which we have permitted the order of the world to creep into the order of the Church. Having gone into the world of nations to make them disciples we have often accepted the order of nationalism, so that we not only remained silent before a nation's pretensions to the status of a chosen people, but have even fostered the illusion with our speech, for instance, about an "American theology" or perhaps even an American gospel in social form, or with our confusion of American and Christian "destiny".[1] In other instances we have so confounded Church and nation that we have regarded the former as an aspect of the latter. Again, the secular order and disorder of economic society have been accepted by the Church and been mirrored in its own order. So feudalism entered into the Church only to be displaced there by the capitalist order of a later time; and this in turn may make way for the socialist order. Whatever may be said for such orders of economic society as containing within themselves for their time and in their times elements of a natural order, the acceptance by the parts of the Church of secular gradations of rank, honour and wealth runs counter to its own order of mutual service. That it should carry out its mission to the men in the middle classes of capitalist society is doubtless a part of the Church's order, but that the mission should result in the formation of a middle-class church which defends the secular outlook and interests of that class is an evident corruption. That this disorder should lead to the demand for the formation of workers' churches which are to represent the secular as well as religious interests of another economic class is intelligible; yet the disorder in the latter case would be as deep as in the former. Perhaps the most painful disorder which has resulted and results from our conformation to the world is present where differences popularly and wrongly called "racial" have entered into the organization of the Church, so that worldly, anti-Christian, white

[1] Note: Many specific examples of this disordering action can be given not only from the pages of theological writings, but also from home and foreign missionary appeals. But in an ecumenical Church each national group can best supply its own specific examples.

and Gentile pride disfigures and profanes the assemblies of Christians, by drawing caste lines even in worship services and at the Lord's Table, and by introducing "respect of persons" even into missionary and educational service.

The disorder in our church relations antithetical to this one is the sin of withdrawal from the world we are commanded to enter. It may be less manifest in external conduct in our day than it was in the days before the great series of monastic reforms and the Protestant Reformation. Yet it is present in other forms, as when we confess our faith only to each other's sympathetic ears in the Church and not before the world, or when we withdraw from the conflict with atheism in the world into our cells for the cultivation of our spiritual life, or when we disclaim responsibility for the political and economic disorders and sufferings of men because the Gospel relates us to another world than this one, or when we consent to the statement that "religion is a private matter".

As for the sin of "proselytism", though we may be inclined to regard the statement of Jesus about the making of proselytes as directed to men of another community than ours, we cannot wholly evade the indictment. We are aware that it has been difficult for us to distinguish between making disciples of Christ and making proselytes, between turning men to the Lord whose cause we seek to serve and turning them to ourselves who serve this cause. We have wanted men to become as we are, because we are Christians, and have confused the imitation of ourselves with the imitation of Christ. So in our relations to the Jews we have virtually demanded their acceptance of that Gentile Christianity which Paul freed from compulsory imitation of Jewish Christianity, while in our relations to the nations of the East we have found it difficult to dissociate our Western patterns of life and thought, of ritual and confession, from the pattern of Christ. Hence also we have carried into non-Christian countries divisions relevant to our culture but alien to theirs, and have with the Gospel exported also our spiritual disorders, and our secular, temporal order which for them has sometimes been a source of disorder.

v

In our repentance we are made aware that all our human

wrongness in the Church is related to a disorder in our relation
to its Head. On the one hand every unbrotherly act of which
we are occasionally or habitually guilty in our relations to other
parts of the Church and to the world outside is also, we must
confess, an action of disobedience to Him. On the other hand
it appears that every such disobedience is evidently rooted in
something wrong in our relation to Him. We disobey Him
because we do not trust Him. In faith we acknowledge Him as
the risen Christ who gives us in our time His order and commandments; in doubt we think Him dead and believe that it is
we who must give others His orders. So we arrogate to ourselves
the right to rule His Church for Him. In faith we are assured
that all power has been given to Him in heaven and on earth
and that therefore we can, as we ought, make disciples of all
nations; in our doubt of His power we adjust ourselves to all the
ruling forces in the world, to the prejudices which hold sway
over the minds of men, to their love of life and of status, to their
worship of civilization and nation. In this adjustment we shift
our faith from Christ to other saviours and other lords, though
our tongues continue to confess His Lordship. In faith we
accept the possibility and the reality of suffering with our Head
and even learn to rejoice in it as a necessary element in our own
and the world's salvation; in our doubt we shun suffering and
perhaps fear even more to lead others into the fellowship of the
cross. Hence our relations to the world are confused and confounded by the fear that we shall suffer if we proclaim and confess Christ before the hard-hearted, the mighty in knowledge or
other strength, and by our anxiety that we may lead the humble
and the weak into increased or additional sorts of suffering. So
we become defensive or withdraw. In our faith we accept His
orders to feed His lambs and His sheep in whatever particular
situation He has called us; in our doubt we question His justice,
fearing that others may receive a more exalted position than we,
and, like Peter, we betray our jealousy of each other by asking,
" Lord, and what shall this man do? "

Thus it is that in the same sphere in which our fundamental
order as a Church appears, our fundamental disorder as members
of the Church also becomes evident. Because we are ordered to
the Head and by the Head of the Church therefore we are the
Church and in the Church; because in this disordered relation
we doubt and disobey our Head, therefore, we are disordered in

all our parts and in all our relations. Hence our sole but also our sure hope of salvation lies not in giving new orders to ourselves or to one another, but in the ordering which proceeds from Him Who rules us and calls us to ever new responses of free obedience. So we say, "Lord, we believe, help thou our unbelief," and in the measure of our faith do in our present what He commands, turning in sorrow from our disordering actions and in joy to His ordering.

2

THE CHURCH OF GOD AMID THE
DISORDER OF MAN

(a) HER WITNESS IN OCCUPIED EUROPE

by Arne Fjellbu

DURING the years of persecution, the Church of Norway was faced with a situation quite different from that which the Church in Germany had to face. In Germany the wave of nationalism rolled along outside the living Church; it was directed to a great extent *against* the Church. The leaders of the Confessional Church of Germany found no support in the national movement, which developed in the opposite direction. In Norway, however, the good national powers joined in active support of the Church and drew from her their strength and inspiration in their national struggle.

In Germany the enemies of the Church came from the people. The ideology and view of life of the Nazis had grown out of the native soil of Germany itself, had their origin in *Blut und Rasse* and *Blut und Boden*; these Nazi theories of blood, race and soil were adopted by the authorities of the State and through them pervaded the whole people.

In Norway, the enemies of the Church came forward and made common cause with the intruders who occupied our country and deprived us of our national freedom and independence. Those Norwegians who collaborated with the forces occupying our country, the Norwegian Nazis, were regarded as traitors, and as such they were despised and regarded with contempt by the majority of the people. From the very outset the Church found it, humanly speaking, very easy to assume its attitude towards the disorder of man—an attitude which proved to be fortunate for it. Practically the whole people sided with the Church. This was a new situation. Though the Church of Norway is a national Church comprising ninety-seven per cent of the total population, and in spite of the fact that the whole people, through religious and moral instruction in the schools, were being in-

fluenced by the Christian faith, the influence of secularism had
been felt for some time. The Church had not succeeded in
counteracting these tendencies. In fact, it must be admitted
that they had infected the theology of the Church itself.

Before the second world war serious attempts had been made
in Norway, as in Germany and other Lutheran countries, to
establish relations between theology on the one hand and
philosophical and scientific investigation and cultural life in
general on the other. As far as theology was concerned, the
result had more often been an adaptation than a conquest,
because people had failed to realize sufficiently that the Church
and theology have a character of their own.

During the inter-war period serious efforts had been made to
maintain the independence of theology and the Church in face
of the world and the cultural and national life of Norway. The
price of this independence, however, was the isolation of theology
and the Church. Co-operating with several concurrent forces,
this isolation forced the Church into a " ghetto existence ", which
gave the impression of a sequestered life. When the last war
came, the Church burst out of this " ghetto existence " and was
suddenly standing amidst the people, with a full understanding
of their problems, national, social, humanitarian and cultural.
The Church became associated with the people as never before.
The concerns of the people were those of the Church. Favour-
able as this position was for the Church, from a human point of
view, it involved a serious problem: did it put the Church of
Norway in a position similar to that in which the *Deutsche
Christen* had been placed when the national ideas overshadowed
the Christian, and the Church became definitely nationalistic
and ceased to be " a Church of God "?

This was not how things turned out in Norway. *Here the
Church associated with the people as the Church of God.* This
was due to the fact that, during the German occupation all the
fundamental human values were at stake. The fundamental
human values, however, are identical with the eternal, absolute
values; and those in question were right and justice, truth,
liberty and goodness, values which Christian influence through
centuries had made the indispensable heritage of our people.

The occupying power did not invade Norway for military
purposes only. The occupants were indeed missionaries preaching a new view of life, a new religion, which they wanted to

force upon the Norwegian people.   Once this was realized, a violent awakening made the people conscious of their Christian heritage.   And the Christian reasons produced for these values rested on such sound foundations that the secular-humanistic view of life was more or less abandoned.   Most people found these values anchored in God.   This being so, their victory was assured.   That is why the Word of God became a living force for many people.   In these circumstances the Word of God became a matter of interest because it held high those values which were at stake.

Of course not everyone saw this clearly.   As a matter of fact not a few regarded the attitude and the struggle of the Church from purely national and opportunist points of view.   In the struggle against Nazism, the Church proved an important and valuable brother-in-arms.   The reasons why the Church entered the struggle were purely Christian ones, vindicated by the Scriptures.   The result produced in the situation in question, however, was a good one.   When waging war, one is grateful to one's allies, even though one may happen to oppose them at some point or other.

With these qualifications, the characteristics given above are correct.   The following declaration by a Communist during the war bears witness to this: "During the war all the 'isms' will change.   None of them will emerge from this war without having been changed, perhaps beyond recognition.   There is only one exception: Christianity, the foundation of which is something objective and unchangeable."

From the very first day of the German occupation, the Norwegian Church was anxious to stand only upon ground proper to the Church as such.   Any action or utterance from the Church would have to be justified from the Bible and from its Christian confession of faith, from its secure position in the words given us through divine revelation.

At the beginning, this resulted in an action which was unfavourable to the national awakening of the people.   In the autumn of 1940 the Nazi authorities decreed that the prayer for the King should be omitted from public worship.   The bishops of the country had to yield on this point.   The reason why this apparently humiliating and compliant decision was taken was that the Church wanted to avoid a conflict with the occupying power on a matter which touched so closely upon the political problems of the country. During the succeeding struggle against the Nazi authorities, the Norwegian Church again and again emphasized that the fight was not political but ecclesiastical, and that the battle-field was that of the Word. In this connection it may be of some interest to stress that, in its fight against those authorities who had caused the great disorder, the Church derived much inspiration from the writings of Martin Luther. His works became a real arsenal of weapons in the struggle of the Church.

This fact may perhaps surprise many non-Lutherans. Luther is generally understood to have preached obedience and loyalty to the temporal authorities. This view has been derived from Luther's idea of " the two realms "—the temporal (represented by the state authorities) and the spiritual (represented by the Church). This idea has been interpreted to mean that each of these realms has its own master, and that two kinds of obedience are therefore called for. According to this, the leaders of the Church might yield to the demands of the secular rulers in all temporal matters, even in cases where they were ordered to perform sinful acts—even the words of Satan. It was considered satisfactory as long as obedience were paid to God and His Word in matters spiritual. Within the Lutheran Church this interpretation has been used to subordinate the Church to the state in a way that has been altogether horrifying.

During the war Luther was discovered anew. It was proved that though Luther preached the doctrine of the two realms, these were both *of God*. Only as long as the authority of a state *considers God as the highest authority* is it in accordance with the Order of God. Melanchthon, the other great Reformer, expressed the same idea in his doctrine of the "two tables". The special duty of the Church is within the first table. The task of the authority of a state is contained in the seven[1] last commandments: " *Magistratus est vox decalogi,*" Melanchthon said. And Luther developed this idea further. Caesar's place is in the second table of the Decalogue. He cannot ascend higher (unless he is led astray by the Devil), but is subject to the commandments of the second table; he is bound to do what God

---

[1] In the Lutheran numbering of the Decalogue, the first two commandments in the tradition of numbering usual in this country are made one whilst the tenth is divided into two. So Anglicans, e.g., would speak here of the six last commandments.

orders, for God alone reigns, and Caesar is not able to alter one single commandment.

Ideas such as these from Luther's writings strengthened the Church of God amid the disorder of man. And imbued with this spirit, the Church felt obliged to maintain the law of God in the face of the authorities, when they trespassed against God's commandments.

In what follows, examples will be given of these fundamental beliefs in the different fields where the Church was faced by the disorder of man.

The first Norwegian institution to break with the occupying power was the Norwegian Supreme Court, the highest legal institution of the country. The members of the Supreme Court resigned as soon as the German intruders usurped the right to appoint members of law courts, in order to make them dependent upon the party then in power, thus violating the independence of justice and the sovereign majesty of the law. There ensued a state of lawlessness in the country. No one any longer felt safe. We were a people whose rulers were no longer a terror to the evil works, but to the good (Rom. xiii, 3). In this situation the Church engaged in a fight of her own for right and justice, for the social order established by God, the Order of God.

A few months after the members of the Supreme Court had handed in their resignations, the bishops of the country sent a memorandum to the Ministry of Church and Education, in which they asked for an unambiguous declaration as to whether the state accepted and felt bound by the judicial and moral obligations expressed in the basic faith of the Church, i.e. in the Bible and in the Creed. "That the state should feel bound by this is necessary from the intrinsic nature of the Church," the letter from the bishops reads.

In a later memorandum addressed to the chief of the Department for Church and Education, the last paragraph reads: "Everyone who instigates evil is under the judgment of God." And in the document proper, fundamental statements such as the following express the view of the Church on the disorder of man: "The Church does not interfere with matters temporal when she exhorts the authorities of the state to be obedient to the highest authority, which is God" (Luther) . . . "consistent with our calling, we urge the rulers of our society to make an end of whatever may be opposed to the holy Orders of God, as regards justice, truth, freedom of conscience and goodness, and we admonish them to build without aberration on the divine laws of life."

During the whole period of occupation the Church, in the same spirit, carried on her fight against the authorities for law and justice in Norway.

Later, when the attacks were directed *against the Church* itself, it had to fight for *the freedom of the Word of God*, for the right to preach in accordance with the Word and its own conscience. During this struggle the bishops issued several pastoral letters which clearly and concisely pointed out the duties and rights of the Church in face of the disorder of man.

The most classical document from this period is one called the *Foundation of the Church*. Among other assertions in the document, the following points of view are maintained: The servants of the Church can only, through the Church, accept instructions as to how the Word of God is to be preached in an urgent situation. The free preaching of the Gospel must be the salt of God in the life of the whole people. The same pastoral contains the following passage: if one kind of régime tries to obtain the position of ruler over another, this is a sin against God, Who is the Lord and Authority of every Order. It is not the task of the Church to hold a position above the state in secular matters. This would be trespassing upon the Order established by God. Similarly, if the state attempts to tyrannize over men's souls and prescribe what the people shall believe, think and feel, this is a sin against God. For if the state tries to force people's souls in matters of religious belief, this only results in pangs of conscience, fraud and persecution. If this is the case, God's judgment spoken in the Scriptures becomes urgent. When the power of the state is no longer founded upon justice, then the state is no longer an instrument of God, but a demonic power. (Luke iv, 6; John xiv, 30; Rev. xii-xiii.)

In this connection the pastoral letter refers to Luther: "The secular authorities may not rule over consciences. . . . If those holding temporal power encroach upon the spiritual rule and try to imprison consciences, where God alone wishes to hold the sceptre, then they shall not be obeyed."

In this fight the Church, faced with the disorder of man, saw these words shining before it: "The Word of God is not bound" (2 Tim. ii, 9) and "We ought to obey God rather than man" (Acts v, 29).

The next sphere in which the disorder of man was made visible was in the attitude of the state to the children and to youth. In the beginning of 1942 the Act of National Youth Service was passed, the purpose of which was to remould Norwegian children and young people on the same lines as the Hitler Youth in Germany. This gave the signal for a fierce struggle, in which Norwegian teachers as well as Norwegian homes made a tremendous effort to save the souls of the young. In this conflict the Norwegian teachers showed how they felt bound by their conscience, and the firmness of the teachers gave strength to the whole people in their fight for our invaluable Christian heritage.

The Church, of course, took an active part in the struggle and made its views clear to the state authorities, as well as to the people. One of the many declarations by the bishops to the authorities reads as follows: "Whosoever by constraint attempts to remove children from the hands of the parents responsible for them, and to infringe upon the sacred rights of the home, will strain the parents' conscience to the utmost. Every father and mother knows that one day they will have to answer to the Almighty as to how they have brought up their children, or allowed them to be brought up. They must always show greater obedience to God than to man."

When the atrocious persecution of the Jews began and once more showed the disorder of man, the Church again spoke its mind in criticizing the evil-doings of the authorities. A letter to Quisling, read from every pulpit in the country, contains the following passages: "The disregard for the human worth of the Jews is directly contrary to the Scriptures, which, from cover to cover, clearly lay down the fact that all peoples are of the same blood. See especially Acts xvii, 26: 'God . . . hath made of one blood all nations of men.' In fact, God seldom speaks more clearly than in this passage. 'For there is no respect of persons with God' (Rom. ii, 11). 'There is neither Jew nor Greek' (Gal. iii, 28). 'For there is no difference' (Rom. iii, 22)." And first and foremost the letter reminds the authorities that when God through the Incarnation assumed human form, He chose to be born in a Jewish home by a Jewish mother.

"According to the Word of God all human beings have the

same human worth and the same human rights. And these fundamental principles the authorities of our state are by law bound to respect. . . . By virtue of our calling we therefore exhort the secular authorities in the name of Jesus Christ, our Lord, to stop the persecution of the Jews, and to forbid the spreading of racial hatred in our country through the press."

These examples of urgent situations may be sufficient to illustrate, within the limits of a short essay, the attitude of the Church amid the disorder of man.

During these times of lupine savagery the Church stood forth as a united Church. An ecumenical movement originated in the period of persecution, uniting the Norwegian Established Church and the other church communities in Norway. The communities of Dissenters, and on some occasions also the Roman Catholic bishops in Norway, fully supported the views expressed in the letters to the state authorities, as well as in those of the Norwegian people. There was also brought about a unification of the divergent movements within the Norwegian Church. *Ecclesia una sancta catholica* was glimpsed, to the glory of God.

One final experience must be mentioned: how the people gathered to hear the Word and to partake of the Holy Communion. The crowding in the churches was partly due to the fact that the Church stood for the national values, that it expressed what no one else ventured to say in public during these years. It may partly be explained by the fact that the Word of God found wide access to the hearts of men and bore fruit there. The increase in the number of communicants, a more general understanding of the Lord's Supper and its place in the Christian community, unity in Christ and unity with one another experienced by Christians during these years—these are the best proofs of this fact.

These years saw also the growth of a greater social responsibility among Christians. Norwegian Christians felt called upon by God to confront the disorder of man with the Church of God.

Times change. The disorder of man, however, continues to be a menace to the future of the world.

The Church of God knows on what foundation it has been built. Valiantly the Church has still to obey God rather than man. The Word of God is not and cannot be bound. But the Church is bound to the Word of God.

And Christ's Promise is heard concerning the Church: "The gates of hell shall not prevail against it" (Matt. xvi, 18).

(b) THE WITNESS OF THE GERMAN CHURCH STRUGGLE

by Edmund Schlink

WHEN an anti-Christian power invades a nation from outside by force of arms, it is a different matter from when it arises within the nation itself, with all kinds of promises which at first it appears to fulfil. In the first case, where it destroys the people's freedom, it is clearly recognized as an enemy; in the second case, where it appears to give the people freedom, its treacherous character is hidden. In the first instance the Christians in their resistance enjoy the comradeship of all who love their country; in the second case the Christians' resistance isolates them from their own people, and they are regarded as traitors to their country. In the first case, resistance is made in loyalty to one's own government against the enemy-invader; in the second case, resistance is directed against one's own government, which has developed into an enemy of Christ, so that painful conflicts break out more and more not only between the orders of these authorities and the commandments of God, but also (as it at first appears) between the divine commandments themselves, i.e. between God's commandment to obey the authorities (Rom. xiii) and the commandment "to obey God rather than men" (Acts v, 29).

Before the Nazis made war on the other countries of Europe, they had already persecuted the Jews and the Church in Germany. They did not do so in open antagonism to Christ, but camouflaged it as "positive Christianity". They did not take action openly as opponents of the Church, but "as protectors of the Church". They did so by using quotations from the Bible, and by claiming to be fulfilling God's commandments. They thus built up an enormous propaganda-machine, which

G

resulted in a general inflation of values, because it sanctified anything it wanted to, so that finally nothing remained sacred. The totalitarian state then went still further and threw its whole weight against the Church, trying to suppress and to destroy it by all kinds of illegal attacks. The Church was not allowed to have any influence on public life, and it was debarred from access to the press and from the use of large halls. Religious instruction in school was either, to a great extent, abolished, or it was robbed of its biblical content. The theological faculties were allowed to atrophy, and the theological colleges were closed. The men and the young people were systematically severed from the Church, and forced into the Party; even the women and children who went to church were watched. The printing of Bibles, catechisms and hymn-books was prohibited, whole branches of church work were forbidden, Christian charity institutions were robbed, church leaders were deprived of their offices, and church order was largely destroyed. Hundreds of Evangelical pastors were taken away from their churches by the state police. Some of them suffered a martyr's death.

The effect of this attack by an anti-Christian power corresponded exactly to what the New Testament prophesies concerning the time during which the Church must undergo persecution.

I

There was a great falling-off among Christians. Many began to be ashamed of the name of Christ, gave up going to church, and instead of baptism, confirmation and Christian marriage and burial, wanted the " dedications " of the " neo-pagan " cult offered by National Socialism. Families were torn asunder: children denounced their parents, husbands opposed their wives, brothers and sisters took opposite sides in the cleavage between faith and error. Love grew cold in many hearts. Its place was taken by delusions and hardness of heart.

This defection occurred not only among the rank and file of church people, but even among the clergy. Many became preachers of the anti-Christian myth and entered the service of the Nazis to replace the loyal pastors and church leaders who had been deprived of office. Many of them became false teachers, and then persecutors of the Church, by proclaiming and denouncing resistance as disobedience to God and hostility to the authorities, and refusing to allow people persecuted by the Nazis to share in the fellowship of prayer and mutual assistance.

But even more shattering than the apostasy, as such, was the way in which it was usually taken for granted, with an easy conscience. When the Nazi philosophy began to influence Christians, many of them did not even notice that all this Nazi talk about "the Almighty" and His "providence" had nothing to do with the Living God, the Father of our Lord Jesus Christ, but that it was directly opposed to Him. They did not notice that the propaganda about freedom, national community, and sacrifice, had nothing to do with God's promises and God's commandments, but that it actually distorted them. It became evident that people were not at all clear about Christian teaching. In many churches, even before the Nazi regime, preaching had become an arbitrary religious explanation of personal destiny and world events. Otherwise, when the crucial moment came, it would have been impossible for a man of our own time to gain such an ascendancy and for him, with his personal philosophy, to become the object of such widespread faith and hope.

At the same time it became clear that the Church had grown much more bourgeois than had previously been realized. People had grown accustomed to regard God primarily as the protector of ordered family life, a help in the education of children, and a friend in the big events of life such as leaving school, marriage and death. He had become the guarantor of national and civic security, in the midst of the insecurities of this world. In many people's minds, Jesus' hard words about what it meant to follow Him had either fallen into oblivion, or had lost their edge. Jesus' challenge to leave one's native land and one's family for the sake of the Gospel, and to choose the way of suffering, seemed strange and remote from modern Christian life. That is why church-goers were surprisingly helpless and unprepared when the persecution started, and they had to choose between abuse, contempt and tribulation for Christ's sake, or rejecting Him altogether. Behind this apostasy stood the failure of Christian teaching which had come to light since 1933, but had a long history; this was why Christians were powerless when the anti-Christian attack set in. To a large extent God's commandments had been severed from the consolation of the Gospel, and were wrongly regarded as autonomous "orders of creation" and political ordinances. The kingdom of this world had become to a large extent either confused with Christ's Kingdom, or else completely cut off from it, instead of the true distinction being made between the two realms both under the dominion of the Triune God. For many people the Church had already become either a function of the state, or a pious ghetto, before the totalitarian state forced it into this position.

So the Third Reich was an apocalyptic experience for the Church and its neo-protestant past, which we shall not soon forget. The breakdown of so many churches was not so much *caused* by outside pressure as shown up by it. The forces at work outside the Church showed up what was real in the life of these churches, and what was only an empty shell. It was impossible to foretell which individuals and which churches would prove to be really spiritually alive in time of persecution, and which would be dead. We found that strong members suddenly became weak, weak members suddenly grew strong; the Church was like a tree, some of whose most healthy branches withered away, while others which seemed almost dead, put forth new shoots.

II

The fact that this apostasy did not cause the death of the Church, but that it received new life, was due to the miracle of divine grace. This renewal began when the Church recognized the enemy's attack as the hand of God, and the unjust encroachments of the state as God's just judgment. The renewal began when resistance to injustice became at the same time an act of repentance and of submission to the mighty hand of God.

Thus through the onslaught of anti-Christian propaganda the Church's ears were re-opened to the Word of God. "It shall be nought but terror to understand the message" (Isa. xxviii, 19). But at the same time God's Word challenged us, questioned the reality of our own religion, and forced us to recognize God simply and solely in His Word. Under the attack of "neo-paganism", but especially through the power of God's Word, its promises and its demands, our usual attempts to see God's revelation in other historical events and forms, ideas and words, save in the historic event of God's revelation in Jesus Christ, completely broke down. Now natural theology broke down; it had assumed a great variety of forms and had been preached as the religion of conscience and idealism, as mysticism and *historismus*, as the religious interpretation of the nationalist past and of the socialist future. Jesus Christ, the Word made flesh, was recognized and acclaimed afresh as the sole Word of God. And one of the strongest Bible movements in the history of the Church has taken place during the last few years in the Evangelical Church, through its new understanding of the Old and New Testaments.

People gathered afresh around the sacraments. The number of communion services and of communicants increased. In the midst of all the tribulation and distress there awakened a new longing for the concrete, personal experience of receiving the body and the blood of the Incarnate Son of God Who has given Himself for us. This destroyed the oppressive solemnity of the memorial services, the form in which the communion services had largely been celebrated. By receiving the body which Jesus Christ gave for us on the Cross, we realized that this same Christ gives Himself to us in the sacrament as the Risen Lord, Who will come again. In the sacrament, through sharing in Jesus' death on Golgotha, we realized more and more that, in this same sacrament, we also share in the great Sacrament to which He will call His own from all over the world, to celebrate it with them in God's Kingdom. But looking forward to His return, we already received the foretaste of the future Marriage Feast which the Lamb will celebrate with His bride, the Church, at the end of time, for ever and ever. These communion services echoed the joy of the early Christians, to whom the body and blood of Christ were objects of the greatest joy and praise.

The Church was again recognized as the meeting-place of believers around the Word and the Sacrament. It is the meeting-place of those who hear and of those who bear witness. In the midst of the collapse of the national Church, and the refutation of the belief that the Church *consisted* of the mass of tithe-payers or of people interested in the Church or of those who were still nominal members, the local gathering of Christians " under the Word of God " assumed a fresh significance. People realized, to their strength and consolation, that the Church was not a mere collection of like-minded persons, but a concrete, local reality. Jesus' promise, that when two or three were gathered together in His name, He would be there in the midst of them, proved to be a great force. So during the last few years the name of " brother " blossomed again, both in the home churches and in those which were scattered, in the prisons and at the front. And the discovery of brotherhood was not confined to one's own confession. Brothers were recognized outside our own confession, where we had not looked for them before, and consolation was found in unexpected places. This discovery of brothers in other Christian churches did not remove the confessional differences between them, but the emphases were changed and opposition paled in face of the reality of God, Who is more gracious and merciful than any dogma of grace.

The liturgy took on a new meaning, after a long period of decay during which the order of service and church worship had become very individualistic and subjective. This break-away from the past occurred in many churches at the same time, quite independently of one another, by the common recitation of the Creed during the service. Then came the special prayers for those in exile or in prison, based on identical prayer-sheets which were used in churches all over the country, and many forms of prayer sent to the churches, expressing in the same words the distress and the thanksgiving of Christians. In this way the upholding power of the common prayer of the brethren was revealed afresh. But the Church is not only a fellowship of brothers, but also a fellowship with our fathers. The Church is one and the same, at all times, as well as in all places. As the isolation of the churches and of individuals increased, the stronger grew the belief in one holy ecumenical Church in all places and at all times; and this certainty sought expression and was strengthened by the increasing use of the ancient prayers of the Church and the psalms, used by Christians at all times. Through these prayers we realized that across all distances and even across the war-fronts, we were *one* people with worshippers in all nations.

The ministry was regarded in a new light. In the local church, it was seen that the first duty, which takes precedence of all other tasks, is to preach the Gospel and to administer the sacraments. But it became especially clear that the Church cannot be led by anything but the voice of the Good Shepherd, as preached in the Word of God. Church government, therefore, must not be left to secular authorities; it is incumbent upon the Church itself, to control its own affairs. The realization that the Church can only be governed in submission to God's Word was preserved in a severe struggle to hold theological examinations, ordinations

and visitations, the burden of which fell mainly on the younger
brethren (curates and assistant clergy) and their families, who
had no security at all.   Through these experiences the opposition between the two possibilities of episcopal or synodal order
lost its exclusiveness and sharpness.   For it became clear that
the office of bishop was different from secular leadership, and
that real synodal government differed in the same way from
political-democratic principles of government.   Moreover, it
became clear that a purely formal, legal authority cannot really
govern a church.

All kinds of spiritual gifts were given by God.   As more and
more the pastors were taken away from their churches by state
expulsions and for military service, the more their congregations
had to face the test of being asked: " Do you believe in God's
promise? "   In this situation many congregations failed.   But
in many churches things were accomplished similar to those
described in Rom. xii and 1 Cor. xii, which had not been
taken into serious consideration since those early times.   Gifts
came to light which may have been present in the congregation
before, under a pastor who thought he ought to do everything
himself.   In some cases the congregation did not receive these
gifts until the difficult times began.   Many elders then began
to understand their task in a new way as that of watchmen.
Many who had only listened to the Word before, now came forward to read to the congregation, or to give their own exposition
of a passage of scripture.   Many, who had never thought of doing
so before, accompanied bereaved persons to the cemetery, so that
the body should not be laid in the earth without a reading from
scripture and a prayer.   In addition to the old office of deacon,
new duties were assumed; readers, catechists, both men and
women, undertook the care of the poor and pastoral work, while
young people taught the children.   In many places the joyful
discovery was made that all gifts can be of service to the community, and that Christ's grace can only be glorified aright
through the diversity of spiritual gifts and services.

The Church realized afresh its responsibility for the world.
The weaker the Church became, the stronger grew its certainty
of the lordship of Christ, the fact that " all power in heaven and
on earth " is given to the Risen Christ (Matt. xxviii, 18).   The
Church began to see the world in a new way, through faith in
the ascension of its Lord; the Church can no longer allow any

realm of life to be a law unto itself; for over and above all human action in every sphere of life, the Church must proclaim the lordship of Jesus Christ. Under the onslaught of the totalitarian state and its claims, the false conception broke down that obedience to Christ applied only to private life. As the totalitarian state no longer recognized any private sphere, the problem of Christian obedience had to be stated in a new way. Since the totalitarian state made use of every sphere of life for its own arbitrary political objects and its anti-Christian ideology, it became clear that not only in family life and in individual religious life, but in the decisions of the judge, in industry, in economic life, in the doctor's treatment of the sick, in the application of military force, and in all political action, obedience to God was at stake—the Lord Who through His death has made everything on earth His own. Hesitatingly, but with growing confidence, the Church in the Third Reich began to proclaim that in every sphere of life we owe obedience to God in Christ, proclaiming its message in face of the world and helping the persecuted. The Church in Germany carried on its struggle not only for the sake of its own existence, but also on behalf of other oppressed races and peoples, whatever their faith.

All this proved that the Church can only help, in the midst of the disorder of the world, by really being the Church. Its most important duty to the world consists in allowing itself to be re-made by the Word of God. When the Church derives its life solely from the Word of God made flesh, the witness of that word within the Church is bound to have effect in saving and bringing order into the world around. But if the Church bears witness to something other than this Lord, however well-intentioned its advice, warning, help and sacrifice may be, it will only increase the disorder of the world.

III

During the last few years the Evangelical Church in Germany carried on its struggle against the anti-Christian power of the state, as a religious struggle. The Church had to decide between decay and renewal. Denial of Jesus Christ meant decay and death. To confess Jesus Christ means life in the Holy Spirit. What were the elements in the Church's faith, which determined what it said and did throughout these years?

The confession of the Church is public witness to Jesus Christ, the Crucified and Risen Lord, as Lord of lords. Confessing Christians declare before the whole world, " that they belong to this Lord in faith and obedience, and wish to remain His, come what will ".[1]

Through its confession the Church rejects the claims of the world and its self-made gods to have any control over it. Confessing the Lordship of Jesus Christ means at the same time unmasking and rejecting the false doctrines of the present day.

Through its confession the Church makes its attack on the world, its ideologies and its self-glorification. The Church's confession is Christ's weapon in His struggle against the kingdom of Satan.

Confession of the Lordship of Christ means at the same time confessing one's own sins. For the Lordship of Christ is the realization of His grace. But how can the Church testify to His grace, to the world, unless the Church recognizes that it consists of sinners who live on this Grace? The Confessional Movement means a movement of repentance.

The confession of the Church makes the One, Holy, Apostolic Church of all times and places real and actual. To confess with our brethren unites us also to our fathers in the faith. In the struggle of the contemporary confessions against the Third Reich, the confessions of the old Church and of the Reformation period received new life. At the Synod of Barmen, Lutherans, Reformed and United, each being loyal to his own confession, made their united confession of Jesus Christ as " the one Word of God ".

The Church's confession is both a witness to the world and a witness in the sight of God; it is not only addressed to the world for God; it is also addressed to God for His own sake; it is therefore both a hymn and a doxology, giving praise for the mighty Act of God. Thus the idea of confession developed in its original New Testament fulness. The Church's confession is always at the same time a witness to the Lordship of Christ in face of the world, a confession of sin, and adoration and praise of God's majesty. The confession must not therefore be understood in its one aspect only, as a new controversial act, or as a never-changing dogmatic possession, or only as a new form of liturgy, or even as a form of church government. If we isolate the

[1] Confession of the Synod of Barmen.

different aspects of true confession the whole confession disintegrates.

Looking back on recent years, the Confessing Church has no reason to feel satisfied with itself. Everything that it did was due to the grace of God. And what at first appeared to be judgment, revealed itself as mercy, as soon as we humbled ourselves before it. The destruction of our earthly supports and securities (which the Church had hitherto regarded as the sources of its own stability) proved to be the grace of God; for we were thrown upon our Lord Jesus Christ. The sufferings of the Church were also God's mercy; for through these sufferings Christ permitted us to share in His glory. He permitted us to experience the greatness of the glory of insecurity, danger, poverty and persecution for the Gospel's sake, and to realize what security is prepared for the insecure, what wealth for the poor, and what safety for the persecuted.

AN ADDITIONAL NOTE

by Reinhold von Thadden (formerly Chairman of the " Council of Brethren" in the Confessing Church)

Professor Schlink's admirable treatment of a vast theme was of necessity so brief as to leave room for two possible misunderstandings. Owing to the slowness of correspondence with Germany, this note is added by one who also took part in the struggle but is now living in Switzerland.

I. It is important to point out that it was not only the Protestants who protested against the pagan views of life and against the wickedness and violence of the Nazis. There was an equally strong opposition from the Roman Catholic Church, as is proved by countless examples of bold outspokenness (e.g. Bishop Count von Galen in Munster), of readiness to accept suffering and martyrdom. But it must not be forgotten that the background and the circumstances of the Roman Catholic Church struggle differed widely from the proceedings in the Protestant camp. The protection of the Concordat between the Roman Curia and the Hitler government delayed the development of events, and

it was not all bishops, priests and lay people who were martyrs
for their faith. Still in the end there were perhaps among the
broad masses of the Roman Catholic clergy and faithful at least
as many resisters as among the Protestants.

It was probably the Catholic teaching concerning the
Eucharist and the fact, connected with it, that Catholics are
accustomed to a life of surrender and sacrifice, which lay behind
the constancy and endurance of the Catholic martyrs that often
compelled our admiration. The Catholic camp was strengthened by the conception of the existence of "natural rights", a
conception which helped the Roman Catholics to nail down the
errors of the National Socialist doctrines.

II. A second misunderstanding might arise if it were con-
cluded from Professor Schlink's synopsis of the spiritual fruits
of the German Church's struggle that the attitude of the Confessional Church, with its Council of Brethren, was the only witness heard during all the years of persecution in Germany. Here
two things must be said:

(1) In the discussions which took place between the Nazi
church of the German Christians on the one side and the church
resistance movement on the other, there was in fact no other
really audible voice which gave the message of salvation in Jesus
Christ and of a real divine community on earth equally clearly
and with the same readiness to take risks. Neither the large
number of neutral clergy nor certain groups among the free
churches dared at that time to say openly to their congregations
or to the world what ought to have been said, and the fact remains that amongst Protestants almost the only ones to show
open opposition were those who had some connection with the
Confessional Church and had accepted for themselves the resolutions of the Barmen Synod.

(2) But one must not at once conclude from this that in the
whole of Christendom there were no currents or movements,
which, apart from the actual combatants, were striving to renew
the Church on biblical foundations, and which were realizing
their object in the face of growing difficulties and threats from
the Gestapo. Here Pietism with its fellowships and its free
churches, the German Student Christian Movement, and the
novel missionary activity of the German "Protestant Weeks"
were as important as the quiet constructive work of the "intact"
churches of Württemberg, Bavaria, etc.

We might call this Christian desire to cling to that which the Bible has taught us a sort of passive resistance, while the Confessional Church had the task of active resistance. But in fact it is not possible to formulate such distinctions without saying something essentially false. So one can only refer to the tragedy of the strained relations for years between "Dahlem" and "The Lutheran Council", which weakened the unanimity of the brotherhood in face of their common foe.

This complex of questions raises the further question how to explain the fact that in the course of years the work of the Church became concentrated more and more on cultivating the inner life. One answer is that every other activity of the Church was year by year to an increasing extent forbidden by the Nazi authorities, most closely watched and pursued by the Gestapo. Finally it was only possible to influence the congregations in the most intimate circles of the Sunday church services and the church buildings, and even there only when the pastor had the courage, as a member of the Confessional Church, to take the risk of exerting his influence. Under these circumstances it is not surprising that there was a steady fall in the number of the more secular listeners on the fringe of the Church.

Further, one must remember that a large majority of the members of the German Protestant Church hardly saw the problem of the significance of the Church for the state and the people as Anglo-Saxons see it, and only extremely rarely took any practical steps about it. Just for this reason one can only say that in a sense the Protestant Church contributed materially to the collapse of the Weimar Republic. Probably in their hearts most members of the Church held "conservative" opinions, and were filled with love of their country and loyalty to the state. But after the First World War the Lutheran, Reformed and "United" (*Uniert*) members of the Protestant Church were certainly ready in all honesty to work with the Weimar Constitution and to take a share in the pacification of the world from inside Germany. As far as I know there were no National Socialists in the Church until the moment they seized power.

III

SIGNS OF HIS APPEARING

———

Volumes I, II and III in this series, prepared for the World Council Assembly, contain a chapter surveying the evidences, from many countries and churches, of renewal in the aspect of the Church's life with which the volume is concerned. Although Miss Wyon has drawn on correspondents from all over the world, such a chapter as this is bound to seem to those who know any region well to have been arbitrary alike in selection and in omission. Only a far longer process of consultation than was possible could have forestalled such criticism. Even as it stands, we believe the picture given to be broadly true and to present by vivid selection what could otherwise be only lifeless generalization.

EVIDENCES OF NEW LIFE IN THE
CHURCH UNIVERSAL

by Olive Wyon

THÉ Christian Church is entering an entirely new period in her history. The Great Century, with its unparalleled expansion, lies behind. No one knows what lies ahead. As the Church moves out into this unknown future, can she discern the Signs of His Appearing? We can begin our study with the knowledge that the most recent period of church history (from 1914 to 1944) has been described, by so great an historian as Professor Latourette, as "one of the great Ages of Faith". In spite of two devastating world wars, and the world-wide upheaval that these have caused or intensified, never before has the Church Universal been so conscious of its world-wide character; never before has it struck root so deeply in the life of peoples outside Europe and America; never before has it been so deeply aware of the sin of disunion, and so anxious to achieve real unity.

It is the aim of this paper to record some concrete "signs" of this new life—if it exists. The weakness, deadness and apathy of so much church life at the present time is only too evident. It would be easy to paint a picture of the Church in grey and sombre colours. In a certain European country, where the Church was in a very low state, the people used to say: "For six days of the week our pastors are invisible! On the seventh they are incomprehensible!" But when we look at the Church as a whole, elements which may seem insignificant when seen in isolation, gain a certain coherence when seen as part of a spiritual pattern which is emerging out of the mists of confusion and disorder. So our record will be something like a picture by Rembrandt: the darkness will be pierced at vital points by Light from above. We do not forget the darkness; but we look thankfully at the gleams of heavenly light; for they are a promise and an assurance that we possess a Kingdom that cannot be shaken.

I

(i)

"If we have got the Living Church, it is easy to put up the buildings!" These are the words of a Chinese bishop, speaking of his devastated diocese, after the close of the war with Japan. To him, in this context, the "living Church" means the "local Family of God", the group of Christians living in a particular place, which meets regularly, as a family, to worship God. Here the Word of God is preached; here the sacraments are celebrated; here is the local "colony of heaven". A "living Church" in this local form, however small and humble in appearance, is an oasis of order and peace in the midst of confusion and disorder, and a centre of light and hope for the whole neighbourhood. One of the facts of the present Church situation is that such churches *exist*. The atomistic individualism of the recent past is disappearing, to give place to something nearer to the New Testament meaning of the *ecclesia* in a given place, whether that be Corinth or Rome, Shanghai, Berlin, or Cape Town, or some remote village in India, China, Africa, or in the Islands of the Pacific.

In China, for instance, in spite of a depressing political situation, and the shadow of famine, the Church situation is full of hope. These local churches have come through great tribulation, and in some instances, of course, there have been losses. But the main note is one of courage and vitality. Only a very "tough" and hardy people could have come through such experiences with renewed life, and an almost entire absence of hatred and bitterness for their late enemy. Report after report comes from China in these terms: "The churches seem to be full of vitality, and are expanding, largely by their own efforts." In one of the poorest districts of Fukien the church life is very vigorous. These people are hardy and virile. They "make excellent pirates, and even better church workers!"

Many churches were cut off from the rest of China for years, and were left entirely to their own resources. From place after place come reports of increased life and vigour during these years of isolation. In some instances this meant there was an increase of forty per cent in the membership of the local churches. Here is the story of one Chinese Church during the war years. It is in the little town of Fukow, in a district flooded by the Yellow River. When the missionaries returned they had to walk for three days over dried silt or along the tops of the dykes above the swirling waters which surrounded Fukow on nearly every side. The town had suffered terribly from war and from floods. But when the English friends reached the mission compound they found a gatekeeper in charge, a clean and tidy mission house, a renovated church building, and a flourishing school for poor children. The church leaders were soon discovered; then their Western friends heard the whole story. When the Chinese Christian elders knew that the enemy was approaching, they decided that at all costs they must protect the church and mission compound. So several of them moved into the mission house, with such of their belongings as they could save from the floods. When all outside Christian activity was impossible they gave themselves to prayer and to Bible study. Some of them learned the Acts of the Apostles and the Epistle to the Romans by heart, and they all studied these two books together. As soon as it was possible they restarted the school; but the church building was in a terrible state, so, after much prayer and discussion, these people (who were already in great financial straits) decided to give a tithe of everything they could sell. They set to work to clean and repair and redecorate the church. Then they reopened it; when the English friends arrived they found the Sunday services in full swing and a crowded church, with many new people being drawn towards Christ.

(ii)

"Worship is the key-stone of order": nowhere is this sense of peace, meaning, significance, experienced so deeply as in the act of corporate worship. A living Church offers living worship. The very existence of Christian worship in the midst of an unbelieving world is like a light in a dark place. An Iranian official recently visited a Christian church built in Persian style: "There is something here that grips my soul," he exclaimed. The Christian architect (himself a missionary) says: "It is difficult to over-emphasize the value of a church in a Moslem land like Iran. To enter a church there is to set foot on Christian soil: to pass from one environment to another wholly different.

There is something about a church where devout worship is offered which differentiates it from all other places."

Worship in the young African churches is still at the experimental stage. Separatist African sects, with their drums and dances and curious rites, make a great appeal, and draw crowds to their services. The dangers of such meetings are obvious, but an experienced European missionary remarks, caustically: "Too much heat is not necessarily worse than excessive cold! "

A Protestant missionary points out that "Catholic" worship, whether Roman or Anglo-Catholic, has a great attraction for the primitive African, and for Christians of the first generation. The services in the churches founded by " Evangelical " or non-episcopal churches in the West, usually reflect the state of affairs in the Home Church, only on a still "simpler" level. The revivalist fire which once gave this kind of worship its real power has died out, and in too many places the result is respectability —and dullness. "Is it any wonder", writes a missionary from West Africa, "that our Christians say, under their breath, or openly, 'What a weariness it is! ' " But there are signs of a new spirit. In Uganda, for instance, where the Church has been established longer than in many parts of Central Africa, there is a deepening sense of worship, and a growing appreciation of beauty in Christian worship. Worship is becoming more closely related to the daily life of an agricultural people. A new kind of service was recently held at the close of the long dry season and the beginning of the rains. The first part consisted of praise and thanksgiving for rain and for water. The second part was an act of dedication. First of all, various members of the congregation brought offerings symbolic of their daily work: soil, roots, seeds, hoes, and laid them before the altar. Then the whole congregation knelt and offered themselves to God for His service.

The same congregation had a memorable Easter Day. Here the growing sense of worship reached its climax. Easter Eve was spent very quietly as a day of preparation, closing with a service late at night in a bare chapel, where the grey stone fabric of a " tomb " stood before the communion table, its entrance closed by a great stone. During the night, a few men and women prepared the chapel for the Easter communion. When the communicants entered the building early on Easter morning, they found the " tomb " open, surrounded by a mass of glowing

H

flowers; while white frangipani blossoms and tiny candles shone like stars on the floor of the sanctuary. The whole service was an act of praise and adoration of the Risen Lord.

One of the most moving instances of living worship comes from the United States of America, from the bogs of New Jersey. This "church" met in a room eighteen by twelve, in a shack that had been turned into a chapel by twelve cranberry pickers. They had come from Florida, where they had been able to go to church. But here in New Jersey, in this out-of-the-way settlement, there was no church and no possibility of public worship. But these men and women were hungry and thirsty for God. So two families decided to live in one room in order to free the other for the chapel. These two families called themselves "God's committee". They cleaned the room, gathered wood, made rough benches, then found volunteers to carve an altar, and a cross upon it. Then they wrote to New York and asked for someone to take their services. A negro minister, a graduate of Yale Divinity School, heard of their need, came to see them, and promised to help them. Someone who visited this "temple in a shack" says that never had he learned more about the reality of worship than in this little community. Above the home-made altar someone had painted a cluster of cranberries, a sign of the dedication of their daily work in the bogs. The service was simple and informal. Negro spirituals were sung; the minister read and prayed, while the people stood with bowed heads in a silence that could be felt. During the sermon questions were asked, and answered. Then a man came forward with two broken bowls, containing Bread and Wine. The Eucharist was celebrated, and Christ came to His people in the Breaking of Bread. This is a living Christian community, and its worship is a token of the dedication of the whole of life—in its hardness and its poverty and its isolation—to the Glory of God.

The keynote of living worship is joy, a joy which breaks out on great occasions. The recent Church Union celebrations at Medak in South India are a case in point. More than five thousand people were present to rejoice over the birth of the Church of South India. Great crowds marched in procession to the cathedral, to the music of village bands, which were making a joyful noise unto the Lord with drums and flutes and cymbals and pipes, and all manner of musical instruments. As the procession drew nearer, the Christian Girls' School started a familiar Telegu lyric:

> O what rejoicing! O what rejoicing!
> Gladness all telling above!
> Jesus our Master our sins hath forgiven,
> For all is the bliss of His love.

This lyric has a tune which sets people dancing in their hearts, and the great procession took it up with fervour. The service in the cathedral was deeply impressive. And at the close, the singing of the Telegu lyric:

> Holy, Holy, Holy, Blessed Lord,
> Can the tongues of purest angels
> All Thy praise and grace record!

lifted all hearts to God.

(iii)

New life within the Church is not only manifested in the regular worship of the local community, or on great occasions. "A rediscovery of the New Testament Church" is also visible in the *liturgical movement*, which aims at renewing the worship of local parishes or congregations within various communions. It is a striking fact that the same urge to revitalize the liturgical life of the Church is present in every part of the Universal Church at the present time: in the Orthodox Church, the Roman Catholic Church, and in many Protestant churches, with their differing traditions. In those churches which possess an ancient liturgy the effort is made to fill the external forms with meaning, and to encourage the faithful to know themselves to be part of the Body of Christ in their own town or village. In the Protestant churches, especially in those which had almost entirely lost all sense of the meaning of liturgical worship, in many countries there is a new movement in favour of liturgical practice.

In France, for instance, the restoration of unity among the Reformed churches has led to a renewal of liturgical life. A new love of the Bible has brought with it a desire for greater reality and beauty in worship. A Commission for the renewal of the liturgy was set up in 1946, and it has already accomplished much. Space does not permit us to describe the work of this Commission in detail, but one point of great importance must be noted: the Commission is quite clear that henceforth the Eucharist must be given its rightful place in public worship, and no longer be regarded as an " additional " service.

This emphasis in the French Reformed Church on liturgical renewal, and on the centrality of the Eucharist, is part of a renewal of spiritual life as a whole. This renewal has three main characteristics: (*a*) the return of the Church to the Bible; (*b*) a new sense of the Church as a divine organism (not an association merely formed by men); (*c*) emphasis on the centrality of the Eucharist.

A similar movement, entitled *Church and Liturgy,* is at work in French Switzerland. The young French and Swiss pastors who are active in these movements feel strongly that " in re-establishing a liturgical framework in their services they re-discover the great commonplace of primitive Christianity, and, at the same time, without ceding anything of doctrine, they arrange new ways of approach to other communions ".

The liturgical movement in the Roman Catholic Church is active in several countries; in Germany and Austria and also in France, Belgium, Italy and Portugal. It has already produced a considerable literature, much of which is welcomed by Protestant readers. Theodore Wedel remarks: " The literature of the Roman liturgical movement reads as if the Reformation had come alive again," for " a New Testament doctrine of the Church, a rediscovery of the meaning of the Church as the Body of Christ, runs through this Movement as a whole ".[1]

On the other hand, while there is a definite desire in some Protestant churches to enter into the ancient heritage of the liturgies of the Church, this movement is not a return to the past. Its leaders realize that " liturgy is a community posses-sion ", and that " only a Spirit-bearing body can create liturgical worship—and only if it lives a life in time ", that is, a life that is fully rooted in the actual life of society, and is aiming at bring-ing the Rule of God into every part of the life of mankind. Younger men and women in the Reformed churches, in par-ticular, are aware that there is nothing archaic in this renewed interest in liturgy. They see it as an answer to the need of the

[1] *The Coming Great Church,* p. 33.

day for living community, under the guidance of the Holy Spirit. They are fully aware that a new liturgical tradition requires an act of creation. As one of them puts it: "We need a modern worship service, a living one, and, after so many 'venerable' texts, a youthful liturgy."

(iv)

The living worship of the Church springs from the living revelation of God in Christ, mediated through the Bible. The Bible is a searchlight in the life of the Church, for it lays bare its sins and failures; it alone can show whether a Church is alive or not. The Bible, which brings the message of God's love for all mankind, is a fire which burns, as well as a balm which heals.

Through all the recent storms of persecution, enemy occupation, war and upheaval, the Church in many lands has learned that its power to endure, to resist all temptations to lower its standard, come from the Bible.

The Church in Germany certainly found the Bible to be its sheet-anchor during the period of persecution. From 1933 to 1938, each year the sales of the Bible exceeded the sales of *Mein Kampf* by more than 200,000. The sale of the Bible in Germany rose from 230,000 in 1930 to 1,120,000 in 1939. This increase was due not only to the experience of the Confessional Church, but to a similar Bible Movement within the Roman Catholic Church. A vigorous Bible work had been going for some years, but the pace was accelerated by the troubled times through which the Church was passing. One feature of this work was the Bible Conferences for priests in which the clergy were taught how to spread the knowledge of the Bible: in 1943 one hundred and thirty-eight such conferences were held. This increased interest in the Bible also helped to draw Protestants and Catholics nearer together in their time of common strain. At one time joint services were held in a Berlin prison by imprisoned Catholic priests and Lutheran pastors, for "the Word of God is not bound".

A return to the Bible is a characteristic of the renewed life within the Orthodox Church in Greece. "Apostolic men" like Makrakis and the Archimandrite Matthopulos based their efforts to awaken new life within their own Church on a deep and prayerful study of the Bible. Present movements, like that of

Zoë (Life), owe their inception to these two men. Among many other literary activities *Zoë* also acts as a Bible Society. It prints the Bible in the original Greek; the New Testament reached a third edition in 1938 with 100,000 copies; the Old Testament (Septuagint) has also been issued in a smaller edition. Another movement which is at work within the life of the Greek Ortho-dox Church is that known as the *Anaplasis* movement. The basis of all its literary and evangelistic work is the study of the Bible led by university professors. In Orthodox Greece to-day there is indeed a "hunger and thirst for the Word of God".

These three examples from Europe could be multiplied over and over again from every continent. In China, for instance, the demand for Bibles has been increasing, in spite of the present difficult situation, and in spite of all the troubles caused by the war with Japan. The life of the Church is being deepened and strengthened by emphasis upon the Bible. All over China new seminaries and Bible schools are being established. In these simple "colleges" the lay leaders of the Church are being trained, while a more advanced theological training is being given in centres of higher education. Roman Catholic scholars are also actively producing Chinese translations of the Psalms and other books; their printing-presses can hardly keep pace with the demand.

In Great Britain, after a period of decline, the tide has begun to turn. There are many societies which encourage the daily reading of the Bible, such as the Scripture Union, the Inter-national Bible Reading Association, the Church Bible Study Union (with members in forty countries), and others. One of the best known is the Bible Reading Fellowship, a movement which began very modestly in a London parish (St. Matthew's, Brixton). The clergy and parish workers came together to see what could be done to deepen the religious life of their own congregation. So in January 1922 the "Fellowship of St. Matthew" came into existence, and one hundred people joined it. In two years there were 300 members in the parish. Then three other parishes joined the fellowship, and the membership rose to 500 at the end of 1924. Then came a time of great expansion: by February 1929 there were 20,000 members; in 1939 there were 238,000. By this time the move-ment had spread far beyond Great Britain. The Monthly Notes were being issued in Mandarin (for China), in Bengali, Tamil, and Arabic.   Australia, New Zealand, and Canada formed their own auxiliaries.   Members are of every shade of ecclesiastical opinion, and although the movement remains an Anglican one, many members and writers of Notes belong to the Free Churches.   During the six years of war there were 98,000 new members.   There are now 6,600 branches and the Monthly Notes go out to 351,000 people.   The leaders can only say with amazement: "This is the Lord's doing, and it is wonderful." They realize that "there are depths of meaning in the Bible that man has not yet fathomed.   The Bible is ahead of the times."

(v)

In life on life the Eternal witness stands,
Enlightenment and freedom in His hands.

These lines from a poem by a Bengali woman suggest the gift that Christ has brought to Indian women.   The actual achievements may not yet be many, but their quality is of a very high order.   From the days of Christian pioneers like Pandita Ramabai, who introduced a ferment into Hindu society which is still at work at the present day, when Indian Christian women are taking a responsible share in the life of their country and of the Church, there can be no doubt that here, in the activity and character of women leaders, is an evidence of living Christian faith which is something new.

In hospitals, schools, colleges, as well as in the directly evangelistic work of the Church, "there is a company of Indian women leaders of quite outstanding ability, devotion and character".   A recent Christian visitor to India says: "Few things in connection with the Church in India were more encouraging and impressive than this."   More and more directly missionary responsibility is being borne by "these Indian women colleagues".   The same writer was impressed by the work of the Biblewomen in South India.   He says: "In many villages I could easily pick out groups of those who have come under their training and influence.   They had a bright and alert bearing that made them quite distinctive."   Women also take a share in "revival" movements: Pennamma Sannyasini, a woman preacher of Travancore, travels about South India and Ceylon, preaching and conducting Conventions.

One of the most recent movements within the Church in India is the establishment of the Missionary Training Centre for Indian Women Workers in connection with the Women's Christian College at Madras. This is a small beginning, but it is full of promise. It "aims at giving women of education and experience a special training that will fit them for the new responsibilities that await them in Church and mission service". Amidst so much wealth of material it is difficult to choose an outstanding illustration of the work of Indian women in the Church, but a particularly characteristic piece of service is that of the Bethel Ashram in Travancore. This Ashram was begun by two women: one Indian and the other English; it has now grown into a resident community of from one hundred to two hundred women, girls, and little children. This Ashram, which is entirely a women's community, is thoroughly Indian in character. It does much good work of a practical kind, and it exerts a creative influence. This is not surprising when we see how much emphasis is laid on prayer and worship. The chapel is the centre of the Ashram. These women know and live by the truth that apart from Christ they can do nothing.

Similar evidences of the value of the service of Christian women comes from China. "The women will be the salvation of China", was the verdict of a foreigner in China some years before the recent war. Now that the curtain has been lifted, and we know what has been happening in China, we can see how great a part has been, and is being played, by Chinese women. Here is a typical instance: during the war a Chinese lady was in charge of a Christian hospital in Hong Kong. She had to handle a situation which often seemed desperate: she endured dangers, privations and humiliations; she and her fellow-workers met this situation with great courage and dignity. Crisis after crisis arose which required the greatest wisdom and tact. She took it all as "part of the day's work"; but one who saw her soon after the liberation of the city and district says: "There are not many stories of quiet heroism in the war to beat it, the triumph of Christian faith over fear and difficulty."

Again, in Amoy the Chinese minister of a large and flourishing church was caught in Manila when the war broke out, and could not get back to China. With the help of an evangelist, his wife carried on his ministry, "undaunted by imprisonment and torture at the hands of the Japanese, and not abating one jot of her zeal on account of her sufferings". In other instances, women with little education, but full of love and zeal, spread the faith wherever they are. In a small market town where there is no church yet, a Christian woman has lived and witnessed to such effect that she has gathered a Christian group of fifty to sixty people from eight villages, as well as from her own little town.

In many countries much directly evangelistic work is being initiated and carried on by women: we have seen that this is the case in India; it is certainly so in China; in France some of the most promising efforts of the French Reformed Church are those carried on by women. They are part of a considered plan to create small Christian communities in working-class districts which will grow into local churches. Thus from the beginning, a team, or a group, lives as a Christian fellowship in the midst of a pagan neighbourhood. These groups are based on a Rule of " prayer, poverty, witness, and work ". One such team settled in an industrial district on the outskirts of Paris; it was composed of three women, a trained nurse, a midwife, and an evangelist. Between them, they earned just enough to carry them through (the "evangelist" did other work in the summer months to enable her to make her own financial contribution to the common pool). After some months, the friendliness and service of these three women had drawn people to them. Sunday services were held regularly: Bible study groups were being carried on; children and young people were coming to clubs and classes. A local church was coming into being.

Evangelistic work within the framework of the Eastern Orthodox Church was begun in Greece (during the German occupation) under the influence of an educated Greek woman. In 1942, Mrs. Chrysanthi Makrykosta, the daughter of a well-known surgeon in Athens, called together a number of women from the upper classes of society, and several men in influential positions. The members of this group took counsel together for the spiritual welfare of their people; they have now started courses of addresses and lectures which are given in the University of Athens, in the Law Faculty, every Sunday afternoon. The movement calls itself the " Christian Corner "; it has districts; everywhere the effort is made to awaken real religious life within the framework of the Orthodox Church. The members of this movement also do a great deal of pastoral work in the hospitals of Athens, and among the numerous patients in the Leper Colony near the city.

It is not difficult to recognize signs of God's working in the freedom and creativeness of Christian women leaders in different countries; but perhaps the most creative and fruitful work of all—in its actual influence—is that of the Christian women who are never mentioned in "reports"; whose names never figure on any lists; the people whom one scarcely notices, and of whom one never hears.   These are the women, often mothers and grandmothers, who live a life of loving thought for others and of unceasing hard work; who train their children in the knowledge and love of God; who lead them into the life of prayer and the love of the Bible.

When the Christian life has almost disappeared outwardly, these women as a matter of course will conduct simple services in their homes for their neighbours and their children.   These are the people who keep the flame of Christian faith burning in the secret of the home.   These women do more for the life of the Church Universal than anyone can imagine.   Throughout the recent war we get glimpses, now and again, of such humble devoted lives.   And we know that this hidden life and service of women in their homes is being given freely and unself-consciously all over the world to-day.   Little is ever said about this service, which is almost more important than anything else at the present time; but reading between the lines of the papers sent in from every part of the world on *The Life and Work of Women in the Church*, we can see that behind it all stands this hidden, devoted, creative life.

In a rural district in Africa there is a Christian Women's Guild!   At a recent conference nearly all the speaking was done by African women, with a freshness, originality, and sense of drama which were delightful.   The whole conference was full of happiness.   These women, and their daughters, have a great responsibility.   Most of the year the men are away at the mines or elsewhere, and "all really depends on the women—the welfare of country and people, and, most of all, the building up of the Church".

A new movement which is full of promise in several countries is the "Christian Home Movement".   The Indian leaders of this movement say plainly "that the Christian home is not the affair of Women's Meetings or Mothers' Unions alone, but that it is the affair of men, women, and children, who, having been placed in Christian families, are privileged to share in the greatest Christian Home of all, the Church Universal ".

An illustration of what these ideals can effect when put into practice comes from South India. In a certain district men and women *together* are co-operating in a spontaneous revival movement. The leaders are a husband and wife from Madras. They work as free-lances, but are glad to co-operate with the churches. " The leaders, husband and wife, work together as one, sharing alike in platform and personal work." Their helpers are being trained on the same lines, husband and wife co-operating in prayer, work and witness. These Indian evangelists lay great stress on the Christian Home. Their work is bearing fruit. " Converts from Hinduism are coming by families ", husband and wife standing together in their new life.[2]

(vi)

A characteristic sign of " new life " is one which is being evoked by the mass paganism of our day. Laymen and laywomen are feeling the need to carry the Christian message and the Christian life into the whole range of their daily life and work. Roman Catholic women are already doing this in a deep and systematic manner through the Grail Movement in Holland and in Great Britain. The new Protestant centres which are springing up in Switzerland (Bossey, Essertines, Geneva), Germany (Bad Boll), France (Cluny), Sweden (Sigtuna), Holland (Driebergen) and elsewhere, for " lay training ", all have the same aim: to proclaim the Lordship of Christ in every sphere of human life, in and through the exercise of one's vocation. Behind all this new movement lies the conviction that nothing but a total Christianity will have any power to combat mass paganism and materialism.[3]

Christian Youth Movements are too well known to need description here. The Oslo Conference of 1947 may be regarded as a symbol of the strength, vitality and promise of these movements which are such a vital part of the life of the Universal Church.

[2] Telegu Baptist Convention.
[3] A brief survey of these laymen's movements all over Europe is to be found in Volume III of this series, *The Church and the Disorder of Society*.

II

One of the abiding characteristics of the Christian Church as a whole is its power of inward renewal. Again and again, when the fire of Christian faith and love is burning low, and the Church seems almost moribund, new movements, led by inspired men and women, have arisen to meet the need of the day. Latourette points out that these unofficial, spontaneous movements, in their turn, stimulate and fertilize the organized church life of the day. To go no further back than the seventeenth century, and to confine our attention to Protestantism, we can trace this line of spiritual renewal from the Puritan movement in England, and in Holland, to the continental movement which may be described by the general term of Pietism, and on to the renewal of the Church of the Brethren, which brought forth the Moravian Church, with its extensive missionary work, and its influence upon Wesley and the Methodist Revival, followed by the birth of the whole modern missionary movement.

(i)

One of the primary forms in which this new life bursts forth is that which is called a "revival" or a "religious awakening", like the Methodist Revival in England at the end of the eighteenth century, or the "Great Awakening" in the Thirteen Colonies of America. The largest revival movements of this kind took place during the nineteenth century, most of them in Anglo-Saxon countries. On the Continent, through the influence of Pietism, a wave of "revival" spread over Western Europe. The result was that "Christianity had a more extensive and a more profound effect upon mankind in the nineteenth century" than ever before.

In the United States of America the influence of these revivals was shown "in the resourcefulness and adaptability of American Protestantism in meeting its varied problems". They also left their mark in the emphasis on the need for personal religion, and in the impulse to social reform which was such a marked feature of American Protestantism in the nineteenth century.

One of the most significant events in the American religious life of the present day is the rise of new sects which "are sweeping across America like a spiritual hurricane". The respectable people in the well-established churches may be "tired of revivals"—especially of a stereotyped and organized kind—but thousands, and possibly millions of people, dissatisfied with the church life to which they are accustomed, and longing for something more vital, have broken away from the larger communions and have founded new sects. This tendency has been intensified by the movements of population during the war. Whenever members of sects from the rural districts moved to cities to earn their living they took their religion with them, and started small groups for worship and fellowship in empty shops or garages or in their own houses. At first the middle-class people in the older churches found this movement difficult to understand, and regarded it as a war-time phenomenon which would fade out as soon as the war was over. Now, however, the movement is being taken seriously, and those who have studied it with sympathy and the desire to understand, see that it bears a striking resemblance to the great evangelical revivals of the eighteenth and nineteenth centuries; they now realize that this is not a wholly new movement, but that it has been growing in strength for the past twenty years or more.

It is impossible to guess how many people are affected by this movement: some would say twenty millions; a careful observer has said from two to three millions. Numbers, however, are less important than the spirit which impels these people, and there is no doubt that there is something vital about them. There is an "eschatological" fervour and glow about these sects. Their numbers grow because they "shout their religion, sing it, pray it, wherever they are—in the factory, field, or on the road". They print and distribute striking tracts and posters; they spend money on broadcasting and on newspaper evangelism before they think about buildings. In one sect alone (Jehovah's Witnesses) 45,000 men and women give part or full-time each week to evangelism by word or tract or open-air preaching.

Of course this emotional kind of religion is sometimes exploited by unscrupulous people for their own ends. But in the main it is true to say that these people are genuine, and that their religious experience means everything to them; that is why they are so eager to share it with other people. "At their best", says an American observer, "the sects have an answer for the guilty feelings of millions of people for whom sin is still a consuming problem." The positive results of this type of revival are evident: a love of the Bible; healing of disease; moral improvement; debts paid.

Many of these sects are very small and meteoric, and these are usually the ones with the longest names: " The Apostolic Overcoming of the Holy Church of God "; " Christ's Sanctified Holy Church Coloured "; " The Pentecostal Fire-baptized Holiness Church ". But there is one, called the " Church of God and the Saints of Christ ", which began in the year 1896, when a man called William S. Crowdy, a Negro cook working on the Santa Fé Railway, had a vision in which God " called " him by name, told him to leave his present work and to lead his people into the true religion. He obeyed at once; went to Kansas and began. Nearly fifty years later Crowdy's work survives in some two hundred churches with 35,000 members. Such an instance reminds us of Ruskin's phrase about " this any place where God lets down the ladder ".

The appeal of these sects is mostly to the under-privileged, the poor and the forgotten. These smaller sects are found in the dingy side streets of the great cities, or in lonely valleys among the mountains of Kentucky and Tennessee—or in the heart of a group of Negro shacks far in the South, or on the coast of Southern California. " Not many wise, not many noble . . ." would serve as an apt description " of all the more sober small sects of America ", says Willard Sperry. Here again we see that " the really creative, church-forming religious movements are the work of the lower strata ",[4] for " the sect is born out of a combination of spiritual and economic forces ". In any case, " the sectarian outbreak of religion ", says a careful observer, " is after all a renewal of vitality . . . in religion and in the Church ".[5]

In India, revival movements occur both within the churches —in the form of large and influential conventions—and outside organized church life in free-lance activities. Some " revivalists " form new sects; others—many of them *sadhus*— go about the country-side preaching and often healing. Historically speaking, revival movements in India and Ceylon owe a great deal to the Welsh revival of the present century, to the Keswick Convention, and to the work of men like Spurgeon, Finney, and Moody and Sankey in Britain and America.

To turn to a very different environment, a revival movement —strongly biblical in character—has been going on in China

⁴ E. Troeltsch.   ⁵ H. P. Douglass.

for some years. It appears to have begun about 1926. It continued to spread through many provinces of China until the beginning of the war. The movement spread from north to south: from Manchuria into Shantung, Hopeh, Honan, Shansi, Hupeh, Hunan, and into other provinces as well, including Fukien.

In Manchuria, in 1933, the Presbyterian missionaries said that in several places "flood-tides of spiritual power have swept people out of the complacency of their former lives and carried them on waves of emotional confession and agonizing prayer into church membership". The leaders were Chinese, both men and women. "Bible classes are full, and meetings are crowded. Dead churches have come to life again." In Shantung a missionary writes: "The revival is a work of God . . . the evidence of changed lives; opium given up, idols torn down, quarrels of years' standing made up, village hoodlums turned into humble men of prayer . . ."

When communication between the occupied part of China and the outside world was reopened in 1946 it was found that this kind of revival had been going on—more quietly perhaps— even during the war. In many places the effects are still evident. A recent English visitor to Amoy found the churches there full of vitality, and obviously still carried on the wave of new life which had been brought to South Fukien some time before by Dr. Sung and other Chinese evangelists. Here is an authentic work of God.

This widespread awakening has already had a great effect on the young Church in China. It has given a great impetus to the tendency to make the Church indigenous. All the committees and conferences in the world could not do what this revival has achieved. Now the Chinese Church knows for itself that "God has visited His people"—where they are; and that they have their own place in His purpose.

The characteristics of this movement are to some extent similar to those in other countries: a deep sense of sin; joy of conversion; love of the Bible. The young Church had prayed for a revival, but it came at first in the form of a judgment on the House of God, and, in its initial stages, it was a very grave and difficult experience. Sins of the past had to be acknowledged, confessed, and forgiven; men and women who had previously felt themselves in no need of repentance now knew that they too were sinners—and this not in a general way, but they saw their need of forgiveness for specific sins of omission or commission. It was very personal; each person knew that God was *there*, dealing with him. It is evident that this is the work of *God*; no human power could have such a cleansing, renewing, effect. The genuine leaders were increasingly driven to prayer; they realized that of themselves they could do nothing. Their experiences led them to the conviction that "when God can get hold of someone . . . to do the work of an intercessor, then He can begin to release spiritual forces for the renewal of His Church".

(ii)

"The fact that to-day we have reached an extremity of secularism suggests that we have reached a new point of departure for religion. Christianity itself is eternally true, but Christianity will have to be positively recreated within the lives of individuals, in terms of personal experience." These words may be regarded as a summary of the aims and hopes of the many small and hidden groups which are springing up within the Church in many lands to-day. What is the inward urge which creates such groups? In nearly every case it is the desire for a closer and more sustained contact with God. Closely allied to this is a deep desire to have a closer contact with one's fellows; to enter into a more living experience of human community. Since the one depends upon the other, it is evident that the impulse is a true one.

Such people, before all else, want to learn to *pray*. They are loyal members of their churches; they have usually "said their prayers" all their lives long; they are regular attenders of the services of their own communion. But their souls "are athirst for the Living God", and so the small, intimate group is born. Natural leaders emerge; and in the course of time a group of "seekers" becomes a creative community. Sometimes such a group is a "cell" within a parish or congregation; sometimes its members belong to different churches in the same neighbourhood. In the intimacy of the group and the common search for better ways of praying and living a new unity comes into being. "I used to be a terrible spike," said an English Anglo-Catholic layman one day, "until I heard a Nonconformist pray—and all my spikes fell off."

Groups of this kind exist all over Great Britain. Most of them are small; and most of them are little known, save by those who belong to them. Periodically their experience is pooled in a conference which has the formidable name of *The Advisory Group for Christian Cells*. Its purpose is well stated in the following paragraph: "There is springing up within the Church, and on the fringes of it, a movement of great promise and vitality. No one is organizing it. It has come into being in response to man's need, and we believe that it is a movement of the Holy Spirit. Its distinguishing feature is that small circles of friends gather together at regular intervals in one another's houses. They meet for prayer, intercession and Bible study, and to plan together for common action." The writer continues: "The ultimate aim is to renew the life of the whole Church. The Church will catch fire when there are enough of these 'living coals'. . . ."

Other similar groups carry on a similar activity: there is the *Fellowship of the Holy Cross*; the *Servants of the Spirit*; the *Society of the Companions of Jesus*; the *"Together" Groups*; the *Fellowship of Meditation*; the *Associates of the Iona Community*; the list could be made much longer; but these few names give an inkling of the kind of spiritual activity which is working like a hidden leaven within the Church, as well as on its fringes, in Great Britain.

In addition to these informal groups which meet in private houses, or in rooms lent for the occasion, small centres are being established where men and women can come away from their work for a few days to pray and talk and think together, in order that they may return with new courage and vision to their ordinary life. The Retreat Movement in the Church of England is an outstanding example of a spiritual activity of this kind, set at the heart of organized church life. Similar houses to be used for retreats, belonging to other communions, have been founded in the United States. High above the Blue Valley in North-east Pennsylvania stands Kirkridge, which is first of all a centre for religious retreat and study, and also the headquarters of "a group of Christians scattered over America and beyond, living under an agreed daily discipline"; it also represents a movement within the Church "seeking God's revival of the Church primarily through the ministry". Spiritually it has many affinities with the Iona community in Scotland. Trabuco, in the hills of Southern California, is another centre "where the religious life is attempted". The building stands alone on the summit of a mountain ridge with a vast view over "waves of tawny hills like lions' shoulders in the sun".

These two centres for retreat and consultation in America are typical of a quiet movement connected with the *Wider Quaker Fellowship* which is fostering the practice of retreats and of serious study of the life of prayer. A paper called *Inward Light* helps to keep the members of this scattered movement together and gives news and results of common experiments. It reports "a growing concern among Friends and others for inner life and growth"; similar movements are: the *Tens* (Methodist) in Mexico and China, and the *Order of the Holy Cross* in U.S.A. At Pendle Hill, the Friends' centre for religious and social study, frequent Retreats are held. A monthly devotional booklet, entitled *The Upper Room*, is produced by the Methodist Church in the United States. Its circulation runs into millions, and it is published in Spanish, Portuguese, Chinese, and other languages, as well as in Braille for the blind.

Permanent centres for Christian life and service which are closely allied in spirit to these Western groups and movements are the Ashrams of India. Here an old Hindu form of religion has been revived and adapted to Christian use. The first Ashrams appeared over two thousand five hundred years ago "as forest dwellings where men devoted to religion lived the simple life, and to which disciples came, not only to receive instruction, but to be trained in the realization of spiritual ideals". Twenty years ago, however, few Indian Christians knew what an Ashram meant. Now they are springing up in many parts of India. Nineteen in India and one in Ceylon are in touch with one another. Six are Anglican; five are Mar Thoma (Reformed Syrian Church); two are Methodist; one belongs to the Orthodox Syrian Church; four are inter-denominational; and one is inter-religious, in which Hindus and Christians co-operate.

(iii)

"Every revival is unlike any other revival. It seems that God breaks out in an unexpected way every time. . . . To those who are watching for the first signs of the coming revival, the omens are convincing, God is going to break out on the land." One of these "omens" characteristic of this "great Age of Faith" is the urge towards Christian unity. This impulse takes many forms and appears in many countries. The first impetus seems to have come from missionary conferences in 1854 and 1860 in New York and Liverpool respectively; the first stage in this movement culminated in the Edinburgh Conference of 1910. The second stage followed, and gathered speed after 1914; its various expressions are usually summed up in the general term, the "Ecumenical Movement", which finally led to the proposal to establish the World Council of Churches: "an organization more inclusive ecclesiastically than any other the Christian Church has ever known" (Latourette).

No great organization, however, will of itself create spiritual unity. Everything depends upon the "seed of unity" being implanted within small groups or "cells" within the local church, and thus working secretly, and often without observation, within the Body of Christ. When such phrases as "the Communion of Saints" or the "priesthood of all believers" begin to glow with new meaning, and to influence the actual church life of a district, this "seed" will grow; it may become a great tree, whose leaves will be for the healing of the nations.

An example of Christian unity in practice, on the local scale, is the parish of St. Matthew Moorfields, Bristol. Here there is "a breath of the authentic fire of Pentecost". The former Bishop of Bristol said once: "People are always asking me to stop things that are going on in Moorfields, but I can't resist the Holy Ghost! " It is indeed largely due to the wisdom and sympathy of this Bishop that this novel experiment has been able to continue. One of its main concerns has been, and is, to carry on the work of the parish as part of a United Front. This means that for the past five years the work of the churches in this whole area of Bristol has been carried on together: two Anglican parishes, three Methodist churches and one Congregational church. Every Tuesday morning, after a corporate Communion Service at St. Matthew's, the ministers of these five churches meet to make joint plans for the work of the Church in their district. This does not mean that differences of outlook and belief are ignored; they are known and respected. But it does mean that "at any and every point where a united witness is possible they try to give it". This is done not merely because it is far more practical and effective, but because the leaders in this experiment "believe that thereby we are living, and can give to our congregations, a Christianity nearer to the mind of Christ than the less dangerous, but not necessarily less sinful, acceptance of the traditional lines of ecclesiastical division".

This group of churches has a United Communion Service once a month, in which, as one of the clergy of the district puts it: "We seek to go as far as we possibly can without abandoning what each denomination has of distinctive value to contribute to the ecumenical Church."

On the large scale, this impulse towards unity has led to a number of actual unions. Several have been in existence for some years; others are being considered. The most recent, and the most striking of these unions is the Church of South India. It is significant because it is the first time that episcopal and non-episcopal churches have united. The fact that "India is a mission-field in which nine of the eleven living religions of the world are found" may have been one of the reasons that has moved the Christian Church in this part of India to lead the way. For a long time past Christian leaders—Indian and European and American—had been accustomed to meet each other every year to confer together about their common task, and to worship together; thus to some extent they had "grown together" before any scheme of union had been launched.

This union is an epoch-making event. It is true, of course, that the act of union ushers in a period of "growing together", and in some quarters has evoked, not welcome, but grave misgiving. A great deal will depend on the success of this venture for the whole future of church unity all over the world.

The ceremony at which the Church of India, Burma and Ceylon, the South India United Church, and the South India Provincial Synod of the Methodist Church, became the "Church of South India", took place in St. George's Cathedral, Madras, on September 27th, 1947. There were 600 people inside the cathedral; outside, a palm-leaf awning had been erected which sheltered another 2,000 persons. At 8 a.m. the first procession entered the cathedral and moved down the nave. The bishops wore simple white rochets with saffron-coloured stoles (saffron is the colour of religious devotion in India). An Indian bishop presided (Bishop C. K. Jacob). The Call to Worship was followed by the singing of the hymn *O God, our Help in ages past*. Bishop Jacob offered the prayer of invocation; then a layman read the seventeenth chapter of John as the lesson. Dr. Wierenga, the Senior Presbyter of the S.I.U.C. (from the Dutch

Reformed Church of America) then led the congregation in a prayer of confession. The Resolutions of the Churches and the Books of Signatures of Assent were then placed upon the Holy Table. There was a deep hush as the three representatives read the resolutions of their churches accepting the Union. Each man in turn went to the chancel steps to read his part. Then each carried to the altar a signed copy of the Basis of Union and the Constitution of the Church of South India. This was followed by a prayer offered by an Indian clergyman. Then Bishop Jacob, standing at the altar, with his pastoral staff in his hand, read the following Solemn Declaration: " Dearly beloved brethren, in obedience to the Lord Jesus Christ, the Head of the Church, who on the night of His Passion prayed that His disciples might be one: and by authority of the governing bodies of the uniting churches, whose resolutions have been read in your hearing, and laid in prayer before Almighty God, I do hereby declare that these three churches . . . are become ONE CHURCH OF SOUTH INDIA . . . in the Name of the Father, and of the Son, and of the Holy Spirit. Amen." The whole congregation sang the *Te Deum*. The work of twenty-eight years had at last come to fruition. A great step had been taken, and " there was great joy in that city ".

The signs of renewal within the Church Universal may not be many, but they are full of promise. In the midst of a world in disorder and despair, these points of light show that God is at work. In the words of Christopher Dawson: " Wherever Christianity exists there survives a seed of unity, a principle of spiritual order, which cannot be destroyed by war, or by the conflict of economic interests, or the failure of political organization." Thus it seems to be the will of God to carry out His purpose of redemption and restoration through " a spiritual nucleus of believers who are the bearers of the seed of unity ". The Church does not know whither she is being led. But as she moves out into the unknown future she knows that she has been given an imperishable " seed " of divine life, to cast into the furrows of this world. In this hope she prays: " Awake, O North wind, and come thou South; blow upon my garden, that the spices thereof may flow out ", bringing forgiveness, healing, and new life to the whole family of mankind.

IV

THE ECUMENICAL MOVEMENT

―――――――

The occasion for the production of this volume was an officially representative gathering of Christians which constituted a new factor in the life of Christendom. So this book ends with a section which considers some of the outstanding questions raised at this juncture in the history of the ecumenical movement. We consider the tension between regional and confessional loyalties within the Universal Church, the growing significance of the Younger Churches in this new fellowship, the causes for the absence from the fellowship of the largest single Christian communion, and, finally, the meaning of this new, permanent organ of the ecumenical movement, the World Council of Churches itself.

REGIONAL AND CONFESSIONAL LOYALTIES
IN THE UNIVERSAL CHURCH

by Oliver S. Tomkins

I THE ROAD TO UNITY

WE seek Christian unity. But when we begin to ask how
we reach it from the positions our churches actually
occupy to-day, the answer in practice is that it is either
through the growing together and mutual understanding of *confessions*[1] or through the closer co-operation of Christian bodies
in a region,[1] sometimes culminating in a regional achievement
of church union. It is interesting that, within the ecumenical
movement in recent years, the trend towards unity has expressed
itself in the Faith and Order tradition primarily in terms of
confessions—how does Lutheranism accord with Anglicanism?
Orthodoxy with Calvinism? and so forth. Regional differences
are only of significance here if they coincide with theological
differences. On the other hand, the more practical aspect, which
is symbolized best by the Department of the World Council for
Reconstruction and Inter-Church Aid, has been a great en-
courager of *regional* agreement. Separated churches in the same
area have transcended their differences both to promote the giving and to administer the receiving of practical help—and often
have found, in the process, that their relationships to each other
are being altered at a deeper level. At the point where doctrine
and practice meet—in evangelism—the ecumenical movement
has hardly begun serious activity, partly because at this very
point the tension between confessional and regional loyalties is
most acute. The practice of "comity" in the mission-field was
not a solving but a postponing of the problem. When the continued existence of comity becomes unbearable (as in South
India) and is resolved in a regional church-union scheme, it
precipitates some acute problems for confessional loyalty.

We all profess loyalty to the Church of our own confession,
which may also exist in a world-wide form. None of us can

---

[1] Problems of *terminology* in each of these cases are discussed in what follows.

escape the demand to express Christian unity, so far as we can, in the various regions in which God has set us to live. The purpose of this essay is to set out, as clearly as its short limits allow, the relation of these loyalties to each other.

In the anomalies of a divided Christendom, the word *Church* is used in a variety of senses. New Testament and primitive usage permit only two. One sense is that of the organically one Body of Christ, the New Israel, to be in which is inseparably connected with being in Christ, in which there are no divisions of race or class but which is set in the world as an earnest of the "age" not of this world. The other sense is that of the *local* manifestations of this one body. In Apostolic times it was often very small, "the Church that is in the house of Priscilla and Aquila" (Rom. xvi, 5); or the Christian community in a pagan city, "the Church of God which is at Corinth" (1 Cor. i, 2). The author of the *Revelation* addresses his messages "to the seven Churches which are in Asia". Any other use of the word "Church" is thus scripturally unsound.

But the division of Christendom has produced three other concepts, of which the word "church" is often used, and by those who use it, with a temporary legitimacy, the regional church, the denomination or confession and (in some cases) the inter-national organization of the confession. These concepts must now be more closely examined.

II THE REGIONAL CHURCH

An early extension of "Church" beyond the strictly local is to the regional, or often national, Church. The latter is an elusive concept, because the concept of nation is itself elusive. *Nations* in some sense are co-eval with civilization: what has given "nations" new overtones in recent centuries is the development of *nationalism*. But long before the development of the nationalisms of the fifteenth and sixteenth centuries, "national churches" had begun to emerge. Their history is complicated. It must suffice here to say that the various racial and regional loyalties of the Byzantine Empire quickly produced "national churches"; that the struggle between Eastern and Western Christendom included a struggle over the legitimacy of autocephalous, regional churches as against the centralized catholicity of the Papacy, a struggle in which both sides overstated their case and left in the late Middle Ages a confused heritage, to which the Reformation was heir.[2]

The common assumption of both East and West since Constantine, that the community and the Church were two aspects of a single entity, was carried over into the Reformation with resulting territorial, or national, churches of varying confessions, Lutheran in Scandinavia and in some German *lände*, Presbyterian in Scotland and some Swiss cantons, Anglican in England. It was chiefly through the rise of Independency in England that a new and sharp distinction between Church and territorial community developed. The strength of the Independent elements in early settlers of North America was a major reason why religion in the United States has never had the pattern of regional associations that characterized Europe.[3]

The theology underlying the various forms of regional church is as complex as their history. Here it is possible only to pick out, in bare summary, some of the theological convictions which are relevant to our inquiry.

(1) The *Christian Empire*: the classical doctrine in the West, following the Constantinian settlement, vindicated the relationship of Church and Empire as two aspects of one whole. One body of men had henceforth two aspects and two governments —a secular government in things temporal and an ecclesiastical government in things spiritual. Thus Gelasius I formulated by the end of the fifth century the concept which was to dominate the whole Middle Ages. Its presupposition is a vast political-cultural unity within which regional or national differences are quite secondary. This concept was never formally abandoned even when the Western empire had long ceased to have the posited cohesion.

(2) The *Christian Nation*: in the greater diversity of the Eastern Empire, nations were a more real fact and Eastern theologians gave them a more serious place in their interpretation of the economy of God. With the development of nationalism in the West, many theologians have found for them a real, but limited, place in the order of creation. The Old

[2] See especially a valuable short historical study, *National Churches and the Church Universal*, by Prof. Dr. F. Dvornik of the University of Prague (Dacre Press, London, 1945).
[3] For excellent descriptive and interpretive articles on this whole question see the essays in the Oxford Conference volume *Church and Community* (Unwin 1937), especially those by Ernest Barker, Hanns Lilje, Manfred Björquist, Stefan Zankow and E. E. Aubrey.

Testament exaltation of the nation has found some very dubious exegesis, but, more securely, on the basis of the total biblical interpretation of history, nations can be accepted as something "given", but transcended and controlled by the Gospel.[4]

(3) The *National Church*: accepting the nation as a part of the order of God for human living, many church traditions have evolved quite clear-cut conceptions of the vocation of the national church. The idea of the "godly Prince" was an axiom of sixteenth and seventeenth-century Christian thought. The modern mind is startled by the completeness of its acceptance. Buttressed by references to archetypal sovereignty in the Old Testament, it found political expression in *cuius regio, eius religio*. It was simply the transference to a different unit of community of the medieval identity of Church and state. Thus Hooker can quite simply write, "in a Christian state . . . one and the self-same people are the Church and commonwealth". On this assumption, national churches conceived their duty to God. In Lutheran terms, the national church is seen as testifying uniquely to the *prevenient* and *universal* grace of God. As Einar Billing wrote of the Church of Sweden, "The one thing we know about every person in our country . . . is that he too is included in the grace of God. . . . That is why we christen our children."[5]

(4) *Establishment*: having its origin in the concept of the "godly Prince", many European churches developed an official relationship to the state, though the details of the relationship vary widely, whereby the state civil rulers *as such* acknowledge the Christian faith, and the Church as such is reckoned (as well as being a super-natural society) to be part of the civil order. But the theological justification of establishment is still vindicated by some theologians, in spite of a complete change in its political forms. To take only one quotation from England, Professor Leonard Hodgson preaching to the University of Cambridge,[6] vindicated the state-connection by appeal to the Old Testament prophets who "spoke as representatives of the God Whom king, nobles and people all professed to worship". Our Lord and His disciples were not *in a position* to interfere as those prophets were—and adds " . . . the witness of the Bible

[4] Cf. the essays by Lilje, as a Lutheran, and by Zankow, as an Orthodox, op. cit., pp. 94-114 and 153-159.
[5] Quoted by Björquist, *Church and Community*, p. 119.
[6] See the *Cambridge Review* 1942, Vol. lxiv. pp. 11-12.

(is) to the truth that only an established Church is in a position to be prophetic." He goes on to point out that after the Edict of Milan in 313, the Christian Church was henceforth in the prophetic vantage-point.

(5) The *two kingdoms*: although Calvinism too has generally welcomed "establishment" in the sense of recognizing its duty to minister to *all* the people, it has often combined this with an affirmation that the Church stood as a kingdom within a kingdom. Andrew Melville in Scotland and Voetius in Holland both contended for the right of the Church to be considered as a free and distinct corporation, with power to decree the constitution and discipline of its membership. The strong, centralized system of the Reformed churches distinguishes their claim for the autonomy of the Church within the state, or indeed (as in Geneva and New England) to establish theocratic states, from

(6) *Independency*: here the governing notion is that of the *gathered* Church in the *local* congregation. But this conception need by no means imply a sense of irresponsibility for the commonweal. In sharp contradiction to the defenders of establishment, both these last two groups would maintain that only a church which owed no kind of dependence upon the state was free to exercise a prophetic ministry towards it. The history of the heirs of the "gathered Church" is full of examples of their valiant exercise of that ministry.

This over-simplified summary of some basic theological convictions as to the relationship of the Church to the regional community makes no allowance for the myriad ways in which theological attitudes have been influenced by political, cultural, economic and other social forces. But however brief our summary it would be inadequate without some indication of them.

(i) *Language* has perhaps been one of the most potent forces in creating a church coterminous with a particular cultural unit. The use of the vernacular in worship has a profound effect on the mind of the worshipper and so deeply affects the cohesion of the Church. The necessity, on one side, for Rome to enjoin the use of Latin to undergird her conception of universality and, on the other, the stubborn persistence of distinctive community-churches in spite of dispersion, as in the Armenian Church and in countless churches transplanted to the United States, illustrate the cohesive power of language.

(ii) *Caste, etc.* Some churches came into existence in a particular caste or economic class and with difficulty, if at all, transcend it. The Syrian Church of South India was, and is, as completely a caste church as the Salvation Army was, and is, a proletarian movement. Such bases of church-community may or may not coincide with regional community and they show an astonishing power of persistence long after the circumstances in which they originated have changed. Most regional areas possess one or more church-communities based on such origins which constitute at least as formidable an obstacle to Christian unity in that area as any doctrinal differences; and the doctrinal differences are rendered more intransigent by the existence of such, often unacknowledged, non-theological factors.

All that has been said about caste, can be true *a fortiori* of *race*.

(iii) *Cultural disunity.* A regional church presupposes a quite highly developed degree of cultural unity in the region of which (in whatever terms) it is *the* Church. Where, because of the size of the region or the newness of its culture or the destruction of its old culture, there is cultural disunity, a regional church of any kind is improbable. It is doubtful whether the United States has yet achieved the cultural unity to make a "national church" conceivable,[7] quite apart from the diversity of the churches there and the aversion of many of them to the idea. We have yet to see the effect of the rising nationalism of the East, with its attendant re-emphasis upon their old cultures, upon the desire of Christians there to achieve a *united, regional* Christian witness. Whilst South India is not a wholly distinct cultural unit within India, the difficulties attending the emancipation of India were often used as an argument in favour of a united Christian Church there.

Enough has been said to show that the *regional church* is a highly complex entity, both in theoretical conception and in historical fact. But the basic idea is simple. Man lives in communities. The small community, within which men can know each other personally, is cared for in the parish or local congregation. The community of mankind also has its proper place in the Christian scheme as the sphere of the Universal Church militant here on earth. Between the two, man's life is also lived in other communities, historically variable and intricately com-

---

[7] See Aubrey, op. cit., pp. 173-174.

posed, but always bearing some relationship to territorial region. The "regional church" is the Christian attempt to bring that form of life, as it must bring all forms of life, under captivity to the law of Christ.

III INTERNATIONAL CONFESSIONS

We must first face difficulties of terminology. We have seen that *Church* has only two fully Scriptural meanings, with "regional church" as a possible legitimate use under certain circumstances. How then are we to describe the various Christian bodies which in fact now exist? Most of them claim for themselves the name of *Church*, some also allowing it to other bodies, according to criteria which vary from the rigour of Rome, which allows it, and then hesitantly, to none but the Orthodox Churches of the East, to the latitude of those who would deny it to none who wish to claim it. But it is certainly used to describe a bewildering range of phenomena. Here we are concerned only to find a suitable word to describe perfectly familiar facts, since to use the word "church" would be a *petitio principii* for many readers. The fact to be described is a community of Christians held together by a common body of doctrine, recognizing a common ministry, having common courts or assemblies for the determination of matters of faith, worship and discipline, in varying degrees having access to common finances, generally (but not necessarily) having a common nationality, the whole bound into a recognizable entity by a common history. This entity we propose to call a *denomination*. Where such a body organizes itself into a relationship, more or less close, with those who share its distinctive theological tenets but are members of other nations, we call it an *international confession*.[8]

The number of denominations in the world is probably uncounted. But since we are concerned here only with the chief

---

[8] Thus, in the use of words adopted here, the Church of Greece and the Church of Bulgaria are "denominations" but belong to the international "confession" of Orthodoxy; the Church of England and the Protestant Episcopal Church of U.S.A. are "denominations" in the Anglican "confession", the Church of Norway and the Evangelical Lutheran Churches in India are "denominations" in the Lutheran "confession", etc. It is a terminology which will satisfy no one wholly, but wide consultation with others has not enabled me to find a better. It is even more confusing when the thought has to be expressed in other languages also!

manifestations of their inter-national organization, we need o
concern ourselves with eight main families. They are: [9]

(1) *The Roman Catholic Church:* organized into some 1,
dioceses. It is by far the largest centralized Christian body
the world, defined by acceptance of the supremacy of the Pa
See.

(2) *The Churches of the Orthodox East:* comprise a family
fifteen autonomous churches, each having its own territorial a
and usually comprising an ecclesio-national entity.   No f
Ecumenical Council has been held since the eighth century.

(3) *The Anglican Communion:* its one effective internatio
organ (though purely advisory) is the Lambeth Conferen
normally held every ten years. The first was held in 1867, a
the eighth is arranged for July and August 1948.

(4) *The Lutheran World Federation* recently held its fou
international meeting at Lund (Sweden) in July 1947.

(5) *The Baptist World Alliance* was founded in 1905 and h
its last Congress in Copenhagen in 1947.

(6) *The Alliance of Reformed Churches holding the Pres
terian System* was founded in 1877 and is holding a coun
meeting at Geneva in August 1948.

(7) *The Methodist Ecumenical Council* is a consultative a
advisory body which held its last meeting at Springfield, Ma
in September 1947.

(8) *The International Congregational Council* was formed
the 1880's; it has recently been reorganized, and its next meeti
is planned in 1949 in Boston, U.S.A.

All these " international confessions ", in spite of their diff
ences, have in common the fact that they transcend nation
regional and racial boundaries, uniting men from every part
the earth in allegiance to certain commonly held convictions
to the nature of Christian truth. Some are more closely bou
to regional origins, though even the Orthodox churches ;
developing in Western Europe and in the United States
Orthodoxy less and less tied to national origins. Some are hig
centralized, and all are gaining in sense of cohesion as mod
means of communication increase their possibilities of cont
Even those which set least store on their world-wide charact
having no interest in exercising dominion over their memb

[9] The writer has given up any attempt to provide statistics. There are sin
no reliable ones available.

faith, do not neglect any inter-national means of helping their members.

IV THE CONFLICT OF LOYALTIES

The only way in which a Christian, in a divided Christendom, can be a member of the One Holy Catholic Church, his faith in which he professes in the Creed, is by being a member of what, in this essay, we have called *denominations* and *confessions*. For some, their confession *is* the Catholic Church. Roman Catholics and, with a different emphasis, Eastern Orthodox, conceive of Christian reunion only in terms of the integration of others into their Church. All confessions believe that, under God, their tradition witnesses to truths which it is their duty not to abandon. All Christians live in " regions " in which they have a sacred obligation to manifest the unity of the Church and to proclaim the Kingdom of Christ. In almost every part of the world the two duties are hard to reconcile.

In this conflict of loyalties, what are the affirmations which might be made in common by all Christians who participate in the ecumenical movement? The High Priestly Prayer of the Lord of the Church (St. John xvii) suggests the two poles between which the life of the Church must be lived. Christ prays for His disciples " that they may be one that the world may believe ", and almost in the next breath, " Father, sanctify them in Thy truth; Thy word is truth ". The life of the Church is to be a *unity* for the evangelization of the world: at the same time its unity is in the *truth*, this truth is itself the Word to which the Evangel witnesses.

Herein lies the justification, in their own spheres, of regional churches and international confessions. It is of the nature of evangelism to be local, concretely concerned with souls in time and place; it is of the nature of truth to be universal, transcending boundaries of time and place.

It is a truism that the " missionary areas " have set the pace in plans for Christian unity, and such plans are always closely related to evangelistic fervour or to the awareness of Christians of themselves as over against an unbelieving world. To seek unity is an inevitable response to a love for souls, not an abstract " love " but love for *these* souls.[10] Their conversion and their

---

[10] Cf. the following essay on *The Ecumenical Movement and the Younger Churches*.

sanctification equally demand it. Precisely because evangelism is concerned with definite locality, regional church unity is demanded; because the Church is responsible to Christ for the common social life of all men, the Church must seek corporately and unitedly to carry that responsibility. These principles remain true at every level of corporate human existence, both strictly local and in regard to the larger community. So long as the nation-state is the power it is in men's lives, so long will there be need for the Church to find forms which are fitted to speak to and act in the nation in the name of God.

But at once the contemporary Christian mind reacts with a caveat. Erastianism is an ugly perversion. Nationalism has so often been the bane of our age that *nationalistic* churches are merely the fortification of evil. Only if national churches are seeking to guard nations from nationalism are they true to their calling.

At this point "inter-national denominations" may speak a relevant word. Every denomination believes itself to be trustee of some *truth*, and, because it is a truth, thereby transcends spatial boundaries. It is because members of the same denomination in different nations hail in each other witness to a truth which unifies them, whilst it separates them from others, that they develop their *inter*-national organization. In each of the cases we have listed, that recognition, tacit or implicit, is the justification for their existence. In none of the cases (except Rome) is there any attempt on the part of the inter-national organs to legislate for or to override the autonomy of their local unity, but, in all, a sense of community in God-given truth is present and that sense is a basic condition for the existence of a "church".

As Erastianism is the corruption of national churches, a magnified *sectarianism* is the corruption of inter-national denominations. A community drawn together by recognition of a common truth is prone to become a defensive alliance against all others. The very process of drawing men together from all over the world on a basis of their distinctive convictions is liable to develop a vested interest not so much in the convictions as in their distinctiveness.

As each of these concepts is liable to its own abuse, so they stand, not in a simple but in a dialectical relationship to each other. There are forms of unity which are perversions of truth.

We dare not forget how in Germany and Japan a totalitarian government attempted to coerce Christian unity to serve its own perversion of truth. It is in the light of such a fate that the development of a " national Christianity " bought at the price of dogmatic integrity, is rightly feared.

There are forms of loyalty to truth which are the enemy of unity. Wherever partial truth is elevated into the whole, where-ever doctrinaire abstractions distract from the love of souls, there unity is threatened. It is the perpetual peril of the life of the theologian and ecclesiastic that he should substitute the tradi-tions of men for the commandments of God.

But in spite of the possibilities of their perversion, both con-cepts have a lawful place in the only policy open to a divided Church. Evangelization and social witness which are regional and concrete, demand unity, regional and concrete, a unity of which the regional church is a proper form. So it is only to be expected and welcomed that in almost every part of the world federations, "councils of churches", and plans for co-operation and even for organic unity are going forward on a national basis and developing with increasing momentum.

But, by an inherent dialectic, the development of "inter-national denominations " has coincided with the development of such national movements. Every one of the eight groups we listed (except the Orthodox, for reasons which they are the first to lament) have held or are about to hold assemblies which symbolize their unity—from the Consistory of Roman Cardinals in February 1946 to the International Congregational Council planned for 1949. Although many of them are modest in their claims, all testify to a truth which they believe to transcend the local loyalties of man, of which they are trustees for all Christen-dom.

Yet neither concept is one in which there is any final resting-place. Above them both stands the One Holy Catholic Church, declared by God, and obscured, even whilst it is professed, by men. Loyalty to *that Church* corrects the errors of the lesser loyalties which are but broken parts of an intended whole. It is not the purpose of this essay to discuss the relation between the " ecumenical movement " and that Church of our faith,[11] but it is relevant to its purpose to point out that in the ecumenical

[11] See the essay on the *Significance of the World Council of Churches*, by Dr. W. A. Visser 't Hooft, pp. 177-193.

K

movement both these concepts already have the context within which they can most fully be themselves and yet avoid their own perversions.

The World Council of Churches is neither a federation of "national councils" nor yet a federation of denominational federations. It is, deliberately and consciously, a council of *churches* in the sense described in this essay as "denominations". For, in the empirical situation, such are the actual entities of Christian organization from which the other two concepts derive. "Churches" in this sense represent the facts; yet as the Council develops it will rightly stimulate its component units in national and regional areas to develop their own co-operation at ever-deepening levels, though in a context in which merely national viewpoints are checked and enlarged, whether among older or younger churches, among established or nascent nations. At the same time it will provide (even in its constitution) for the corporate contribution of the great distinctive Christian traditions, not in order that they may harden into rivalry but that they may be mutually enriching. Truly regional churches are needed, and will be needed for so long as men's lives are lived under strong regional influences of whatever kind; international confessions are needed until their limitations are transcended in a wider unity, and such truths as they guard are universally recognized. But such loyalties ever live under the threat and the promise of the Living God Who calls us to unity in the truth.

an invitation to join the Church. " Is the challenge of the Gospel
to India fully declared unless all the time it is presented as
including, in the directest possible way, a challenge to join the
organized Church of Christ? " asks Dr. A. G. Hogg in his recent
study on *The Christian Message to the Hindu*. " And must not
the command ' Follow Me ' have as an intrinsic part of its meaning a summons to join His New Israel—that Church of which
He . . . selected the first leaders? " And Hogg goes on to add,
" Whether or not this note was insufficiently stressed in the
preaching and teaching of my contemporaries on the Indian
mission-field, I have to make regretful confession that it had
very little place in my own teaching. This was because, until
almost the end of my missionary career, the idea of the Church
was no intrinsic part of my conception of the Gospel."

It can be said with little fear of contradiction that what makes
the primary difference in outlook between the leaders of a
previous generation in the younger churches and those who are
the leaders of to-day (both local and foreign) is that they perceive
no mere " consequential relation " between Gospel and Church
but a relation which is both " integral and constitutive ". Undoubtedly this changed understanding is due to the influence
of the ecumenical movement on our thought-life. In the early
days of the movement towards church union in South India the
dynamic came from two sources: one was the practical necessity
for co-operation, forgetting our differences, so that we may more
effectively and economically carry on the evangelistic task; the
other was the drive of a blind sentiment based on the swell of
impulsive feeling which refused to admit that Christian unity
can permit differences.

As the negotiations for union in South India proceeded, the
ecumenical movement in the older churches gathered force. We
profited by your studies and conferences. We came to a fresh
understanding of the biblical basis of the Church, of the
historical traditions connected with various denominational
views concerning the ministry, and we realized the significance
of the symbolic rite of the sacrament of the Lord's Supper as a
ratification of the essential unity of all believers in fellowship
with one another and with the Head of the Church.

Now that the Church of South India is an accomplished fact,
we look back with thankfulness that in all our travail to interpret locally in the life of the Church in South India the

ecumenical oneness of the World Christian Community, we had kept the following ideals firmly in view: (1) The unity of the Church is organic. (2) It comes about in the actual process of growing into unity. (3) It is possible to comprehend and include all that is valuable and worth preserving in the different denominational traditions. (4) A transitory period of adjustment and " irregularity " is inevitable.

In both the younger and older churches there has been a manifest desire to work for unity. But while we talk in terms of " unity " in the hope of a future good to be realized, you of the older churches invariably think in terms of " reunion ", with your minds retracing the past history of divisions hallowed by the memory of saints and martyrs. This seems to be a fundamental difference in outlook. It is responsible for your emphasis on a "federal basis" of union while our insistence is on "organic" union. In the immediate years to come, as the younger churches grow in strength and influence and as they become more and more independent of their connection with the older churches, this difference in outlook and objective will become pronounced.

Paradoxically enough, one of the blessings of the ecumenical movement in the older churches is the fresh discovery that many devout men and women have made of the significant values contained in the traditional teaching of their various denominations. It is true that there has been a clearer conception of the Church. But alongside of this there is growing self-consciousness of the denominational churches too, and in some cases Christians of a denomination with large membership in different countries have come together to form world federations and ecumenical conferences. To us of the younger churches, it is passing strange that with the spread of the ecumenical movement, and frequently as a direct consequence of it, many smaller sects and sub-denominations have now become prominent and active participants in the national councils of churches in countries like Britain and the United States.

This revival of denominationalism concerns us vitally. Many small missionary societies from the lands of the older churches, sponsored and supported by some one or other of these minor denominations, feel justified in starting evangelistic work in areas where the younger church is moving towards organic unity. They tend to counteract what seems to us progress towards unity.[1] This anomalous situation can be very distressing in areas where "missions" supported by funds from abroad and "churches" directed by local leadership exist side by side.

As indicated in a previous paragraph, the younger churches are in various stages of development, even in the same country. In the "mission-stage", where the primary emphasis is on evangelism of the non-Christian and the nurture of the infant community of converts, denominationalism has no place whatsoever. One of the important lessons of missionary history is that as evangelists we cannot afford to be denominational. It is in the "church-stage" of missionary history that we tend to become conscious of denominational teachings. The evangelist's message is universal; the minister of a church instructs his congregation concerning the special teachings of his denomination. We look to the ecumenical movement to help ease the transition in our development from the "mission-age" to the "church-age"—and it seems so clear to us that only if we keep in view the hope of a church organically one can we effect a right transition from "mission" to "Church".

In South India, for instance, another complication arises. Not only do we have denominational churches in this area, but also a fairly large section of the Eastern Orthodox communion in Travancore, referred to in general as the Syrian Church. They are a sadly divided community. Apart from the Uniat-Syrians, there are two main sections of the Syrian Church—the Orthodox Syrian Church and the Mar Thoma Syrian Church. Within the Orthodox Church there are two main parties—the Patriarch's party, which owes allegiance to the Patriarch of Antioch, and the Catholicos' party, which recognizes a local Catholicos as its administrative head. Besides, there is a section of members of the Syrian Church which forms part of the Anglican diocese of Travancore and Cochin, which was one of the four dioceses to be included in the Church of South India.

At the time negotiations were started for union in South India, the Mar Thoma Syrians were thinking of joining in the scheme as it took clearer shape. The spread of the ecumenical idea did not only effect a revival of a healthy denominationalism (like everything, liable to be abused), but also a new interest in Eastern Orthodox churches. The many Orthodox communions

[1] Cf. the preceding essay on *Regional and Confessional Loyalties in the Universal Church.*

in Europe and the Middle East were thus quickened to a new sense of importance. To us of the younger churches it is very clear that these Orthodox communions will not easily give up their separate identity even within the ecumenical fellowship. In India, on the other hand, it seems unfair to encourage these Orthodox communions of the Syrian Church to persist in division. They might have eventually formed part of the new united Church if it were not for the revived consciousness of separatism that the ecumenical movement has paradoxically enough engendered.

There is one important point concerning the significance of the ecumenical movement about which the younger churches would desire clarification. A good deal of confusion is caused by the easy way in which the term "ecumenical" comes to be applied. Any inter-denominational undertaking, for instance, is described frequently as "ecumenical", especially where the project is taken up by several denominations, each retaining its separate identity, and yet all working together for a common end. No one can quarrel with such a use of the term, for it does connote that outlook of fellowship and sense of unity which characterizes the coming together of churches of different denominations.

But it is also true that the term "ecumenical" denotes a number of churches of different lands, each with a culture all its own. So that the world community of Christians in their ecumenical oneness would bring together in multiform grandeur, into a single rich mosaic, the varied culture-patterns characteristic each of the national and racial groupings into which we Christians of the world would seem to be divided by the very order of creation. To us of the younger churches the national expression of the common faith is a precious possession. Not a little of our energy in the infant church in our midst is employed in exploring ways and means of making it indigenous to the soil. We hope some day that the younger church, each in its own land, will prove worthy of its cultural heritage and national genius.

The ecumenical movement which seeks to unite the Christian peoples of the world into a sense of togetherness ought to be both inter-denominational and inter-national. To us of the younger churches it is the inter-national nature of our faith that strikes the imagination; to you of the older churches it is the inter-denominational character of ecumenical Christianity that compels admiration. After all, you do not differ so widely among yourselves culturally, and your present history has drawn you all so much more closely together that there is a vague fear (why not be frank about it?) amongst us of the younger churches that in a World Council we may lose our national identity and cultural uniqueness, being dominated by the sheer weight of your collective strength and cultural homogeneity.

Perhaps this is one reason why we have greater loyalty and affection for the International Missionary Council than for the World Council of Churches at this stage in the progress of the ecumenical movement. To us it is vital that ecumenical Christianity be both international and missionary. We are concerned seriously with the fact that church-consciousness and mission-consciousness have not always kept together in the recent development of the older churches. The ecumenical teaching in regard to inter-denominational fellowship evokes great enthusiasm. But the challenge of the missionary cause as an ecumenical task does not seem to meet with the same response.

Earlier in this paper reference was made to a signal contribution that the ecumenical movement has made to the younger churches. It brought us the conviction that the relation between Gospel and Church is not merely consequential, but integral and constitutive (to borrow the telling words of Dr. Hogg). What the ecumenical movement has not yet brought home to the older churches is this same truth, only expressed in terms of relation between Church and Gospel. Interest in missions is not derived from enthusiasm for the Church; both proceed from fidelity to the Gospel, the faith once for all committed to the saints.

Many leaders in the older churches are already conscious that if the ecumenical movement is to make a real impact on the life and thought of Protestant Christendom everywhere, it ought to keep in view the ultimate goal of the organic unity of the Church universal and catholic; it should be increasingly alive to the international and inter-cultural nature of the ecumenical faith as it is to the inter-denominational and inter-church nature of the world community of believers; it should quicken ever anew the missionary nature of the faith so that the integral and constitutive nature of the relation between Church and Gospel is pressed home to the Christian conscience.

This contribution is written from the background of the author's own situation, that of the Church in South India. Other areas might have stressed other aspects of the relation between the ecumenical movement and the younger churches. Space prohibits a truly representative survey of the outlook of the younger churches unless it were to be of a very vague and sketchy kind. We have preferred to let a single representative speak in concrete terms of the situation he knows best, though it has meant omitting interesting material from other areas.

EDITOR.

3

THE ROMAN CATHOLIC CHURCH AND THE ECUMENICAL MOVEMENT

(a) by K. E. Skydsgaard

I

T HE most difficult front in ecumenical work is beyond any doubt the relationship to the Roman Catholic Church. One might be tempted to say that the difficulties here are so great that any relationship at all is rendered impossible. It is an ever-recurring sentence when the ecumenical movement is under discussion, that "all church communities are represented *with the exception of the Roman Catholic Church*". Is it therefore possible, when talking about the relationship between the Roman Catholic Church and the ecumenical movement, to say anything else than that there is no connection whatever between the two?

The purpose of the following pages is to show that the matter is much more complex than is generally supposed.

In the ecumenical movement we may distinguish between three tendencies. The foundation for any kind of ecumenical activity lies in the acceptance of the bitter and tragic truth that the unity of all Christians in one visible body has been shattered and that, instead of their common cohesion in one outwardly visible Body, many Christian bodies do in fact now exist, not only side by side, but often in fierce opposition to one another. It is just because the various communities are beginning to realize that this separation is a sin and an affliction, which is obviously contrary to the will of Christ, that there is to-day an ecumenical movement. In this bitter recognition of facts all churches agree—including the Roman Catholic Church, which perhaps feels a deeper grief over the disunion and dismemberment than many other churches.

This basic recognition is the first point. The second trend is a divergency in the interpretation of the unity of the Church, an interpretation which naturally also has a practical influence upon ecumenical work. In the non-Roman Catholic churches the interpretation varies and may lead to conflicts. We only need to mention the interpretations of the Church and its unity by the Greek Orthodox, the Anglican, the Lutheran, the Reformed, and other Protestant churches. But the differences of opinion on this question between these churches have not been able to prevent them, on the whole, from joining in the common ecumenical movement during recent decades, culminating in the setting up of a World Council of Churches.

For there is also this third feature of the ecumenical movement, that the churches are moving out of their isolation into active co-operation, not only in matters of practical concern, but also in order to get closer to one another in questions of faith and teaching. In many cases the different points of view give rise to conflicts and difficulties, but behind it all there is a common will for mutual understanding and thorough discussion of the problems which are the cause of the difficulties. It is here that the Roman Catholic Church has felt that it must call a halt. It shares in the grief over the divisions among Christians and it is deeply interested in the unity of the Church, but its own interpretation of this unity not only differs so widely on important points from that of the other churches that it is not able to join in the efforts, but must even insist upon a definite and uncompromising "No". We only need to mention the encyclical *Mortalium animos* (1928) in which Pius XI definitely prohibited any Roman Catholic from taking part in ecumenical meetings. "Thus, Venerable Brethren, it is clear why this Apostolic See has never allowed its subjects to take part in the assemblies of non-Catholics."[1]

Protestants often accuse the Roman Church of narrowness and sectarianism, of ecclesiastical arrogance, and spiritual imperialism. And it cannot be supposed beyond question that such factors have not played a part in the attitude adopted by the Roman Catholic Church, both on the part of individual theologians and of papal proclamations down the ages. It is often an impossible problem to reconcile the words, and also the spirit, of the official proclamations with the ecumenical leanings and sympathies of many individual Roman Catholic theologians.

However, it would be a serious mistake to content oneself with

---

[1] *True Religious Unity*, Engl. trans. of *Mortalium animos*, p. 20 (Publ. by the Catholic Truth Society, 1928). See also *Codex juris canonici*, Can. 1325, para. 3.

such a reaction to the position of the Roman Catholic Church. It would, in spite of every difficulty, constitute a far too cheap and easy solution for the non-Roman churches. The attitude of the Roman Catholic Church must be explained from far deeper and more essential factors, as is now being realized much more widely than previously. When Rome contends that the unity of the Church is not a goal lying ahead, but something which *has* already been made manifest in the Roman Catholic Church itself, because this alone is the Holy Catholic Church, and thus alone the Church of Jesus Christ, and when it further contends that true reunion can only take the form of a reintegration or reincorporation into this unity,[2] this is not, on her part, the expression of some kind of spiritual imperialism, but the expression of a particular conception of the nature of the Church and its unity. If, therefore, we are to come to a real understanding of the unsympathetic attitude of Rome to the ecumenical movement we must try to probe into this basic point of view.[3]

But even though we want to try to penetrate into the deepest motives lying behind the refusal of Rome to join in the ecumenical movement, and by doing so, to respect and perhaps also understand its attitude, will not the result be, nevertheless, the same as before, that between the Roman Catholic Church and the ecumenical movement there can never be any connection? Shall we not, in spite of consideration and sympathy, be forced to say that *here* the ecumenical movement has reached its absolute limit?

The question is this: Are the other churches to be content with the answer officially given by Rome, and consequently to regard all ecumenical efforts from Roman Catholic quarters as irrelevant private efforts which have no foundation in the Church itself and which must therefore be regarded with the greatest reserve? The answer to this must be an emphatic " No! "

So far as I can see it is not sufficient in these matters to abide by the more or less official statements, both previous and contemporary. The papal decrees, even where they are most

---

[2] " There is but one way in which the unity of Christians may be fostered, and that is by furthering the return to the one true Church of Christ of those who are separated from it " (*Ibid.*, pp. 20-21).

[3] A very clear explanation of this view is given by M. J. Congar, O.P.; *Chrétiens désunis. Principes d'un Oecuménisme Catholique*, 1937, pp. 63-148; Engl. trans. (Bles, 1939), pp. 48-115.

explicit, do not express the whole attitude of the Roman Catholic
Church on this question, just as, for instance, the condemnation
of a Protestant doctrine does not contain the *whole* attitude of
the Church to Protestantism.[4] Therefore: the exclusive study
of the *Mortalium animos* would not be sufficient to obtain a
really clear conclusion, as it is chiefly directed against the
ecumenical movement in its first inadequate and groping
attempts, an inadequacy which is now also felt by many leading
theologians in the other churches. That Encyclical is definitely
in opposition to the ecumenical movement which found its
expression at Stockholm in 1925 and may not be—and actually
is not, even in the Roman Church—taken as covering everything
which the Roman Catholic Church has to say in this matter.[5]

Here, as always when we are trying to understand the nature
of Catholicism, it is not enough to study only official documents,
but we must force our way into the living theological and
ecclesiastical tradition as expressed in the whole spiritual life of
the Roman Catholic Church.

We cannot set our minds at rest with the thought that this
problem has been solved once and for all. It is obvious that the
ecumenical question is not seen in the same light by the Roman
Catholic Church as it is by the other churches; this does not
mean, however, that it is of *no* consequence whatever to the
Church of Rome. It is also true that the ecumenical movement
here actually reaches a boundary line, but it does not mean
that this boundary is to be absolute—only that in this case other
methods must be employed. What would be the sense of an
ecumenical enterprise which had not at least the intention of
including the largest of all the Christian communities? If it
had not, it would instantly cease to be ecumenical.

The question then is this: How is ecumenical co-operation
between the Roman Catholic Church and the other Christian
bodies possible to-day? And: How does the Roman Catholic
Church itself regard the possibilities of such co-operation? The
reply to these questions is closely connected with the relationship
between Rome and the other churches. And here we must make
a distinction. Its relationship is not the same to the Greek
Orthodox, to the Anglican, the Lutheran and the Reformed

---

[4] See, for instance, L. Lambinet, *Das Wesen des katholisch-protestantischen
Gegensatzes*, 1946, p. 208.
[5] Cf. Congar, pp. 179ff. (Engl. trans., pp. 116-144); also an article by Charles
Boyer, S.J., in *Unitas* (Vol. II, No. 4; Dec. 1947; publ. in Rome).

churches, not to speak of all the other larger or smaller church communities. The order in which these churches are mentioned signifies an increasing degree of difficulties in mutual relationship. In the following pages we will primarily consider its relationship to the Reformed churches, more especially the Evangelical-Lutheran Church.

I am well aware what influence this limitation in point of view will have on the value of the present paper. Thus it will hardly be possible to avoid the difficulty that, for instance, American readers will find very little which bears upon their problems, just as members of the Anglican, not to speak of the Orthodox, Communion may be justified in feeling that their attitudes have not been expressed. However, it will be difficult for any member of a particular church to express adequately the problems of other churches. For each individual church has its own, often very complex, problems in this field. I hope it will be possible, even from this more limited point of view, to minimize the "limitation" by treating the matter in such an inclusive and general way that it may be of interest also for others than members of the Lutheran Church.

II

During the course of the centuries an essential change in the relation between the Church of Rome and the Evangelical Church has taken place. It is best understood by contrast with two attitudes which, although still to be found, belong essentially to the past. The first might be called the attitude of *confessional polemics*. At this stage, each side assumes that it fully understands what the other side means and is only concerned to refute it. Although the motive was the defence of truth, the method of assault from embattled positions led to polemics rather than to mutual respect. By reaction, there next emerged the attitude of *confessional irenics*,[6] which also assumed that positions on both sides were known and fixed, but that they merely represented a beneficial variety of outlook within the infinite range of truth. The works of Schleiermacher admirably illustrate this relativist attitude.

[6] I here take the word "irenics" in another sense than the one in which it is used in the "irenical method" as described by Dom C. Lialine in *Irenikon* (IV, 1938, p. 4). On the contrary, the thought expressed there corresponds in several ways to the third standpoint which I describe.

But theology is a question of *truth*, not of points of view. Although at many points widely apart, these two attitudes are paradoxically alike in one regard, they both assumed that the relationship between the two confessions was known and unalterable. So both are fundamentally non-ecumenical.

In opposition to these two attitudes, there is now a third, which is finding new ways and is opening up new perspectives; this view will undoubtedly have a more and more decisive influence on future developments.

In order to understand it I must draw attention to individual factors which have contributed to the fact that Roman Catholicism and the other churches have moved nearer to one another. I shall mention three, the first two of a more historical, the last of a more theological nature.

In the period following the Reformation, Catholicism and Protestantism were separated from one another, not only religiously, but also politically and culturally. To be a Catholic or a Protestant meant not only that one had a different faith, but also that one had a different political opinion, and a different culture. *Cuius regio, eius religio.*

Later a change took place. Both the Age of Enlightenment and Romanticism brought the two parties closer together, not in faith, but on the purely humane-cultural level. In the Romantic Period a cultural sphere was created, supported by Catholics and Protestants alike. The difference between these two Confessions became more and more a purely religious contrast. From a merely external, sociological point of view, Catholicism and Protestantism are to-day compelled to live side by side in the same sphere where both Roman Catholic, Protestant and atheistic forces make their influence felt, in spite of the fact that Catholicism to-day still strives to create its own cultural and political sphere. It is a fact that the relationship between Catholicism and Protestantism varies very greatly in this common sphere. There are places where the relationship may be rather strained, not least where a politically defined Catholicism attempts to make its influence felt, and at times exerts strong pressure on an Evangelical minority. The relationship may also be difficult where Catholicism exists as a missionary church in countries with a predominantly non-Roman Catholic Christian population.

On the other hand, it must be emphasized that Roman

Catholicism and Protestantism have been drawn closer together, by common struggle and distress, into a common front against the anti-Christian powers of our times. We are in the midst of one of the great decisive epochs and transition periods in the annals of humanity, a period in which old things are dying and new are being born, a period in which everything is characterized by anxiety and pain, dissolution and a watching for the new which is to come. At such a time it is not strange that the Christian churches should draw nearer to one another and should be more intent upon what they have in common than upon what is separating them. When there is danger and distress things may happen of which smug self-sufficiency does not feel any need. When one's house is on fire one does not feel like continuing an old quarrel.

At such a time there is a possibility for ecumenical work for which the previous ages did not give occasion. One is simply forced into it. It may prove that behind greatly dividing formulations there is, nevertheless, a unity both in regard to the view of man and his relationship to the various earthly spheres of life in which he has been placed, and with regard to essential points in the Christian Faith. There can be no doubt that developments during the past few years in the Western countries have played a very great part in the change of relationship between the Roman Catholic and the Evangelical churches. We only need to remember the relationship of the two churches under Nazism.

The Evangelical Church also has its history. It will hardly be possible to maintain that the history of the Evangelical Church is a blameless one. The Reformers denounced the Roman Church for having muddied the pure waters of Revelation with the traditions of men. Now Protestantism must confess that the philosophy of liberalism and the conclusions of biblical critics, in their extreme and irresponsible form, sometimes betray the principles of the Reformation.

In this respect the theology of Karl Barth has had a decisive influence. His uncompromising attitude towards the Roman Catholic Church has not prevented him from regarding it as a very serious challenge to the Protestant Church. "Here", he says, "in the Catholic Church there is an ecclesiastical substance, a knowledge that the Church is the house of *God*—corrupted,

L

unrecognizable substance perhaps, but nevertheless not lost substance."[7]

Finally a third and last reason should be mentioned for the
changed relationship between the Confessions. To the same
extent in which Protestant theology again turns towards the
Reformation and in renewed sincerity enquires into its mission,
to the same extent we shall once more come face to face with
Catholicism, and the latter with us. As long as we only met
Catholicism with the accusation of being a religion of hierarchical authority or a mystical, magical sacramental religion,
Catholicism probably heard nothing but the questions of modern
emancipated culture. It was a query *from outside* only, not
from *within*, i.e. from a church which declared itself to be
standing on the ground of the Bible and the Creed. It was not
the same question as was set out in Luther's 62nd Thesis:
*Verus thesaurus ecclesiae est sacrosanctum evangelium gloriae
et gratiae Dei.* The new hope in the situation to-day is that
the Catholic-Evangelical discourse is now possible as a real
theological and ecclesiastical discourse.

III

We have now come to the point where we may repeat the question already previously asked: How is ecumenical co-operation
between Roman Catholics and Evangelical-Lutherans possible
to-day?

Students of Catholic-Protestant relations differ in their estimate of the relationship between the official utterances of the
Vatican and the more co-operative attitude of certain Catholic
groups and individuals. But Catholics of the latter kind would
emphatically deny that their action implies any kind of dis-
loyalty to the Holy See. Perhaps the soundest interpretation of
the discrepancy is to see a distinction within the Roman Church
between what can be safely said *coram populo*, which is always
extremely reserved and, indeed uncompromising, and the liberty
of action which authority is content to allow to groups and
individuals whose fundamental principles are judged to be
wholly sound and reliable. The Roman Church *as such* is
wholly uncompromising and yet, where more flexibility appears,
it is no less truly part of the life of the same Church.

[7] See *Der römische Katholizismus als Frage an die protestantische Kirche,
Zwischen den Zeiten*, 1928, pp. 224 onwards.

It is of very great importance that the ecumenical movement should realize this standpoint and act accordingly. Thus great misunderstandings and difficulties can be avoided. The meeting between Roman Catholicism and Evangelical Christianity can only be a meeting between individuals or groups of individuals from the different communities. It is here that the ecumenical work between the two parties must take place, but on the other hand, it is here that it is possible. *This* is where, for the time being, the effort must be made.

The most important part of this work is *prayer*: "*ut omnes unum sint*"—"in such a way and at such a time as God wills it", as it is phrased in the literature of the *Octave of Prayer for Unity*, that remarkable movement associated with the name of the Abbé Couturier of Lyons. Earnest prayer on both sides must be the basis for all ecumenical work.

There is, further, *active co-operation in practical matters*, e.g. co-operation on social questions, and in opposition to wrong political interference in education, the family and the professions, which has been definitely encouraged by the Popes in recent years.[8]

Added to this comes the *study of the Bible*. It is remarkable to note how widely Catholic and Protestant scholars have come to agree in their interpretations of Holy Scripture during the last twenty-five years, and a widespread movement to encourage Bible-reading is in progress in the Catholic Church.[9]

Finally, the *common theological discussion* of controversial matters, in periodicals like *Catholica* (which is temporarily suspended), *Irenikon, Dieu Vivant, Unitas* and others, and through personal contact. This last approach has been practised to a great extent in the *Una Sancta* movement, which became very widespread during and after the war, especially in Germany, where theologians and often also laymen gather together for frank and fraternal discussions of questions concerning faith and order. The great material which very likely is to be found here should be made the subject of thorough investigation. This new co-operation is based upon two points: First, the two parties are both included in the *Una Sancta*. This sen-

[8] See especially the Pope's Christmas Broadcast, 1941; the Foundation of *Unitas*, announced by Vatican Radio, 11th July, 1945, and the Encyclical *Quemadmodum*, 1946, appealing to all *Christians* to help children in distress after the war.
[9] See the account of it in Suzanne de Dietrich, *Renouveau biblique* (Edition Oikumene, Geneva, 1945), pp. 271ff.

tence will be understood differently by Roman Catholics and Protestants, but it is, nevertheless, possible that the two parties can acknowledge their oneness in this common assertion: "On both sides we are included in the Church of Jesus Christ."[10] To deny this would be to deny the reality of Baptism. The condition for a real ecumenical co-operation is that the two sections of Christendom do not begin by denying this fellowship, this one-ness in *Una Sancta,* visible in our common Baptism and, in spite of all, in our common Creed: *Credo in Iesum Christum, filium Dei unigenitum, Dominum nostrum."* This unity is something which is bigger and stronger than all differences and contrasts, because it does not originate in something human but in God Himself.

But secondly: In this very unity the differences become evident, differences which are not of peripheral importance, but are concerned with the most vital part of the confession of the common faith. A difference which does not penetrate to the very core of the matter is of no importance. The acceptance of this difference on vitally important points is a condition without which ecumenical discussion will lack sincerity and reality.

In admitting the tension between these two poles—one-ness in faith in Christ on the one hand, and the contrast in matters of faith of vital importance on the other—all ecumenical work must be carried on. This tension must be endured and not be neutralized by false compromises or be neglected through the one party feeling superior to the other in self-sufficiency.

The question then is *how* this work is to be done. What is needed first and foremost is that this radical change of heart on both sides, now confined to a few, should become general.

It is one of the great misfortunes, due to long separation, that a widely differing mentality has been created. The contrast between the two churches is not only a contrast in the way in which the great Christian questions are being answered, but also in the very manner in which these questions are being asked. In the course of time certain established and almost insurmountable prejudices have grown up on both sides which assert themselves with the certainty of an axiom whenever Catholics and Protestants speak, either about one another or to one another.

[10] As to the interpretation of this sentence on the Roman Catholic side, see, for instance, Congar, p. 278, and Rademacher; *Die Wiedervereinigung der Kirchen,* 1937, pp. 15 onwards.

There is here a feeling of resentment which must be energetically stamped out.

On the basis of such a change of mentality, a new discussion must and can take place between Roman Catholics and Evangelicals where the fundamental issues may be debated, not as "controversial matters" where it will once more—although perhaps in a more friendly manner—be a case of defining what is truth and what is heresy, but in such a way that the two parties may state their position to its fullest limits and as concisely and copiously as possible, and in such a way that the other party will actually *listen* to it.

In order to achieve this it is necessary that the two communities study one another's theology, and try to find out the principal and central motives. This will have the result that the theological discipline called "symbolics" will receive a new aspect. It will not, as hitherto, be only polemical, nor merely a descriptive historical science, although it must always rest upon thorough historical studies, but it becomes the theological discipline in which the individual Confession, so to speak, leaves its own sphere of living and enters into a direct contact with the other Confessions. In this way "symbolics" becomes the self-critical conscience within the individual Confession, in which it regards itself in the critical light of the other Confession, while at the same time feeling the necessity of its own questions relative to the position of the other party.

A further important feature of the spirit of impartiality in which such a discussion must take place is the *demand for truth*. It must not for one moment become a matter of obscuring all that which each side has accepted as being the truth, and there can be no thought of working out a more or less artificial formula of unity on any point. An accepted point can only be abandoned when that which a church has been teaching, or has neglected to teach, proves to be in disobedience to Christ Himself. This is to state that both Catholics and Protestants must place themselves under the authority of the prophetic and apostolic teaching. They must both be under the sovereignty of the revelation of God as found in Holy Scripture. When the individual churches begin to ask themselves if this or that teaching is truly in accordance with the Word of God, ecumenical work has already begun. For in so doing, a spirit has been created which does not agitate for its own infallible opinions, a spirit which is not obstinate and quarrelsome in sticking to its own, once-for-all adopted opinions, and which is not ashamed, when the occasion arises, to let itself become convinced by clear reasoning, because truth is greater than opinions and personal pride.

Now the objection may be made that this spirit may *perhaps* be possible in the Evangelical Church, but that it is impossible *on principle* in the Roman Catholic Church. The Evangelical Church may possibly accept a question from the Roman Catholic Church directed to itself, but the opposite is unthinkable beforehand. From a Roman Catholic point of view, a discussion must always aim at proving to the Protestant the inner untenability of his whole perception. It is beyond any doubt that great difficulties will arise here and, nevertheless, we on the Evangelical side must be aware of various signs which clearly indicate that on the part of Catholicism also a new attentiveness is awakening, an inner investigation, a self-criticism, not of the Church as such, but of the exact form which the Roman Catholic Church has taken in the course of its empirical development, in which restrictions and prejudices have occurred, so that truly Catholic thought (which in this connection means the whole and undivided Christian truth) has had an incomplete development. The same is the case when it is said that the Roman Catholic Church, in order to be truly catholic, lacks something which now exists outside its limits in the other Christian bodies. Protestantism possesses genuine elements of truth which have not found expression in the Roman Catholic Church. And even though the latter may add that what Protestantism contains of actual "catholic" matter can only find its true and complete expression in being transplanted into the bosom of the Roman Catholic Church, there is in this view a self-criticism, a frankness, and a responsiveness which at first sight seems astonishing to a Protestant who has already long since formed his final opinion of the Roman Catholic Church.

If we study Catholic theology to-day,[11] dealing with these questions with an open and attentive mind, we should be startled time after time by the frank willingness to admit that "catholic" was often turned into "catholitical", and that often the opposition to one or the other controversial opinion forced Roman

---

[11] See, for instance, Congar, pp. 30 onwards; Lambinet, pp. 207 onwards and Rademacher, pp. 39 onwards. Collate also R. Grosche: *Pilgernde Kirche*, 1938, J. Lortz: *Die Reformation in Deutschland*, and O. Bauhofer: *Einheit im Glauben*, 1935.

Catholic theology into a one-sidedness, not only with regard to the individual theologian, but also in the ecclesiastical definition of doctrines as evidenced in *Enchiridion symbolorum*. Catholicism is something far greater than the anti-Protestantism which is threatening to become the all-deciding factor in post-Reformation Catholicism and to make of the Roman Catholic Church "a fortress almost as much as a Church" (Congar). From the Evangelical side we must not misunderstand this, and must not draw light-hearted conclusions from it, but on the other hand we must not be ignorant of the fact that here something is happening, and must refrain from giving it a false and unsympathetic interpretation based on preconceived ideas.

In this new mentality and this new objectiveness the present view on the relationship between the Roman Catholic Church and the Evangelical Church differs widely from both the polemic and the irenic standpoint. In this spirit the discourse demands a real effort and study of the great fundamental issues: Holy Scripture and Tradition, Church and Ministry, Word and Sacrament, Justification and Sanctification, the real meaning of the Gospel and of faith in Christ. The more the two churches, each in its own sphere and according to its own light, probe into and live according to the truth about Christ, the more we may hope that the final and surviving unity will emerge *in spite of all*.

IV

I began by saying that the most difficult front in ecumenical work was the relationship to the Roman Catholic Church. The thoughts put forward on the previous pages have not aimed at weakening this assertion. On the contrary!

Ordinary ecumenical co-operation between the churches must go on without the participation of the Roman Catholic Church and probably also be the subject of much criticism and antagonism from many quarters in the Catholic Church. The Pope's Encyclical with its definite refusal to join in this work still holds good.[12] Nevertheless, something new is emerging. Therefore

[12] On this point it is interesting to compare what two commentators, one from Evangelical and one from Catholic quarters, think about this question.

The Evangelical commentator: "*Mortalium animos* represents not only the official doctrine, but the working policy of the vast machine, and, while I am most eager for every kind of personal understanding with persons, I suggest that

the result must be that even here on the most difficult front, where apparently irrefutable reasons speak against it, an ecumenical activity is at work—perhaps in a way different from that manifest in other places, but equally important.

To the above, which has been only briefly outlined, it might with good cause be asked, as it actually has already been asked, "What is the value of these contacts between Roman Catholics and other Christians which are essentially contacts between religious individuals and groups, meeting on a common plane of mystical experience?" The answer to this question must in the first instance be the not very positive one: Of how great or how little value this co-operation will be it is impossible to-day to determine with certainty. Everything is still in its beginning. But it should be emphasized that that which to-day takes place quietly *may* some day break through and be of an importance at which we at this moment cannot guess.

Meanwhile it is imperative to work, to watch and to pray for the unmistakable signs which, in spite of all preconceived opinions, nevertheless have appeared on both sides.

Finally we must realize that, even though it may be considered beforehand to be a rather "impossible" enterprise, it is nevertheless certain that it is the road which we must follow at this moment, although the way ahead may seem dark and obscure. Often a traveller must follow a certain path without knowing exactly where it may take him. He must do it because he knows that, in spite of everything, this is the path *he* must take at this point. Thus it is also in the relationship between the Roman Catholic Church and the Evangelical churches. Even the contrasts in all their profundity will in God's good time illuminate the eternal truth.

the World Council should, in general, rest their relations with the Vatican on the assumption that *Mortalium animos* represents their view and policy still."

The Catholic commentator: "To tie up with *Mortalium animos* is not advisable, nor to *Codex juris canonici Can., 1325, par. 3*, which forbids religious discourse with people of other faiths. The widespread *Una Sancta* movement in Germany shows that since Pius XII this canon is evidently no longer in force." The commentator thinks that the encyclical of Pius XII *Mystici corporis Christi* (1943) gives a far better basis for a real dialogue.

(b) *A Supplementary Note by a Roman Catholic Writer: Fr. Maurice Villain*

WHAT does the Roman Catholic Church think of the ecumenical movement? What is she doing, and what is she capable of doing on its behalf? Such is the question.

The classic reply is well known. . The encyclical *Mortalium animos,* of whose decisive conclusion Professor Skydsgaard has reminded us, would seem finally to preclude Catholics from any active collaboration in the work of reconciliation between Christians such as is conceived by the ecumenical movement. Rome, it is said, has once and for all condemned, even in principle, pan-Christian conferences.

We are grateful to Professor Skydsgaard for having interpreted this document of the first importance with a more discriminating eye, and also for having generously exonerated Rome from the charges of pride and imperialism which on this account are so often directed at her. The attitude of Rome is, as a matter of fact, governed by her own conception of the Church. Her consciousness of being the authentic visible society established by Christ has always been part of her faith; she professes that the ecclesiastical body united to Christ since Pentecost has never been able to renounce Him, in spite of the stages of its development (which are precisely the law of its life), in spite of the very grave crises through which it has passed in the course of centuries, in spite of the moral failures of its leaders and of its members. Its apostolicity is a historical gift; its personality—and consequently its internal unity—cannot in any circumstances be lost. That is why the Catholic Church, in her official documents, regards the unity of Christians as being a step of re-admission into her fellowship; that is why she is seen to distrust the compromises which seem likely, in however small a degree, to stand in the way of the constitutional principle which is her flesh and blood. Hence her severity towards the pragmatic ideas of Stockholm (this is said with full recognition of the nobility of the enterprise of N. Söderblom, who was, moreover, extremely far-sighted, and made more dogmatic claims than the bases of the *Life and Work* conference would lead one to suppose); hence her reserve, now as in the past, towards a congress which seeks gropingly the "body" in which the spirit of unity, in labour everywhere among non-Catholic Christians, may ultimately become incarnate.

Many are astonished, many are shocked. For my part I shall simply confess that I have more than once asked Protestant friends: "If, in the face of such tentative efforts, and, up to now, of such uncertain results, you had been Rome, what, then, would you have done?" There has been an instant's reflection, followed by the hesitant but unmistakable reply: "We would probably have waited. . . ."

This Professor Skydsgaard perfectly understands. And how grateful we are to him for having made his readers feel the extent of the tragedy which this dualism of positions involves for the future of Christian unity: for showing them how painful it is for the Roman Church to be unable to overthrow the barrier of her own constitution (and of her faith) in order to go to Christians who—as many besides herself know—positively need her if their labour is not to be in vain. Who, henceforth, having weighed the extreme gravity of this point of conscience, can speak in irony?

Yet Rome is acting.

Her silence, to begin with, which is itself a witness, carries with it its own efficacy. I do not speak in paradox, but because that is my conviction after having studied the rising tide of big conferences. Has not Rome's silence played a part in directing the ecumenical movement towards dogmatic essentials which could not be clearly perceived in the engagements so nobly and generously entered into at Stockholm? From the first appearance of *Faith and Order* at Lausanne, it orchestrated—if it may be put so—the demands of Anglicans and Orthodox for a more constructive theology of the Incarnation and the Sacraments; it stimulated Protestant researches into the structure of the Church as an apostolic-hierarchical institution; and what doubt can there be that one day it will pose this very serious question as being one of primary importance?

But furthermore, Rome brings to the ecumenical movement above all the collaboration of her prayers. When in 1908, in the Episcopal Church of America, the *Octave of Unity* was instituted, bishops were to be found among us who adopted it. Moreover, it was a French priest who, in 1937, effectively extended its audience to world-wide dimensions, in the new formula of the *Week of Universal Prayer for Christian Unity*. Discretion prevents me from being more explicit, but one would do well to reflect on the spiritual contribution made by the little tracts of Lyons which, each year, stimulate the intercession of Christians, both Catholic and non-Catholic. Between the feasts of the Chair of St. Peter and of the Conversion of St. Paul (January 18-25) they are all bidden to kneel together, to repent together, with one voice to ask of the Father of all "the Unity which Christ wills, and as He wills". Our appeal was heard, the cry "Awake" has little by little reached all the corners of Christendom, and no more is needed but to draw the net tighter by a combined and persevering effort. The World Council is assuredly the first body to profit by these earnest supplications; besides, has it not admitted as much since the *Faith and Order* movement joined in observing this Week of Prayer? And it is in truth in this perspective that we must see the message of Mgr. Charrière, Bishop of Lausanne, Geneva and Fribourg, to the World Council in February 1946 through an intermediary, the Swedish Lutheran Bishop Ingve Brilioth; we read there this sentence: "While you are met together at Geneva to concern yourselves with this essential problem (Unity) my prayer goes up with yours, in union with the one which Jesus made on the eve of His Passion . . ." Is this not the sign of a new spirit?

How, after that, could our Catholic activities, steeped in an atmosphere of such spiritual density, fail to find what Father Congar calls the "ecumenical dimension"? True, all ages are not propitious to it. At the beginning of the twentieth century, for example, the Modernist peril, which the Church was not yet prepared to master, forced Pius X back on a narrowly traditional position. But this very concentration made possible the germination, in the following age, of many prophetic seeds whose flowering we are witnessing to-day. In this general task of "taking stock of our resources" of which the pastoral letter of Cardinal Suhard, *Advance or Decline of the Church* (1947), is one of the most authoritative and optimistic testimonies, I should like at least to stress, as falling exactly within our subject, the renewal of biblical studies. If Rome's silence seems to our Protestant brethren to raise the question of the Church as a community, their attitude to Rome seems to raise for Rome the question of the Word of God. Now to this fundamental question the

biblical renewal is an active answer. The task will be a long
and exacting one, because it is not enough to possess scholars
trained in the best disciplines; we need in addition and above all
a clergy so conversant with the Scriptures that the whole range
of its teaching is nourished by them, and that it is zealous to
communicate to the faithful the taste for them and their daily
practice. Not until then, to use a happy phrase which pastor
Arnold Bremond has made his own, will the Mother Church
have discovered anew her "biblical milk".[1] Besides, the
encyclical of Pius XII *Divino afflante Spiritu* makes this a duty
of the clergy, and outlines the methods to be used.

There remains a long series of facts and indications which
taken together can help us to pass a judgment on certain profound trends, virtual rather than clearly declared, of the Catholic
Church.

A book could be written tracing the graph of Rome's attitude
towards the Orthodox churches, but I must for lack of space
confine myself to a bare enumeration. We can first of all
record a progress, within the last eighty years, in the papal
documents: from Pius IX who was content strictly to recall the
rights of the Roman Church—to Leo XIII, who was the first
to advocate the study of Eastern history and theology—and to
Pius XI above all, who laid stress on the obstacles of a psychological nature which history had piled up in the path of
rapprochements; and on this matter he allowed it to be understood that the Catholic Church had to examine its conscience
and to admit reforms. We might also note the creation, in the
last twenty-five years both in and outside Rome, of technical
institutes—universities, colleges or monasteries—for the study of
the languages, theology and liturgies of the East, and the
establishment of an annual *dies orientalis* in all seminaries, in
such a way that now the spirit of Orthodoxy is present in the
Catholic Church. In another connection, centres such as the
priory of Amay (at Chevetogne in Belgium) or Istina (at Paris)
are extremely valuable for meetings of theologians. But how
much we regret, on both sides, that political pressure constrains
the Patriarchal Church of Russia to decline the advances of the
West!

Although it is here much more reserved, the attitude of the
Roman Church towards the Reformed churches is not at all

[1] *Edifier l'Eglise*, Delachaux and Niestle, 1945, p. 102.

the systematic refusal that one might imagine. Witness the colloquies, which are becoming more and more numerous and well attended, between Catholic and Protestant theologians—spiritual meetings in the form of retreats, intellectual meetings, or better still both at once, when study is illumined by prayer; meetings which are never secret but always authorized by the diocesan bishop or by the superiors of the religious orders; meetings which are no longer tentative, as are those which occur at the outset of such a difficult experiment, but properly conducted, here and there at least, by a precise method, put to the test in specialized groups (for the Catholic theologian has now at his disposal an approach appropriate to researches of this nature). Here are loyal exchanges of views on all subjects, including the extreme points of our divisions; a unique field of investigation for the understanding of mentalities; detailed information on the principles, the constituent parts, the vocabulary of our respective religious traditions; constructive essays grounded in the original sources and dealing with the true pivot of problems, so often unbalanced by " this besetting fever which the spirit of the Counter-Reformation has imposed on Catholic thought";[2] times of recollection, of fervent resort to the Spirit when, at sore points, cries of *Non possumus* are uttered.

Such is our modest work. It is in truth only laboratory work, limited to relatively restricted groups; but we believe ourselves able to affirm that it goes deeper than does the work of large official meetings, and that these meetings will themselves one day benefit by it.

Is there any need to recall also that an ecumenic literature, already quite important, has appeared among us, springing either from the general stream of theological studies, or from more particular experiments of which I have just spoken, or on the occasion of Weeks of Prayer. To the articles quoted above, let me add the following reviews, which are wholly concerned with questions of reunion: *Irénikon, Russie et Chrétienté, Catholicité, The Eastern Churches Quarterly, Unitas,* etc., and the collections: *Unam Sanctam, Ad Unitatem, Théologie, Sources chrétiennes,* etc. We owe, finally, a special reference to the *Una Sancta* movement, taken in hand by the conference of German bishops at Fulda.

[2] A. M. Roguet, O.P., preface to *La Clef de la Doctrine Eucharistique* of Dom Vonier, Lyons, 1943, p. v.

The objection may be made that the Catholic Church is absent from these labours, since she does not commit herself by any official step. This is to fail utterly to appreciate her behaviour. As Professor Skydsgaard well understands, the action of the Catholic Church goes beyond her own documents (which are, especially on this subject, very rare, and show moderation, for the use of the flock whose faith they seek to preserve); it includes in reality the whole area of her tolerations and safe-conducts. We must remember that we are here in the midst of prophetism. Prophetism ordinarily appears in the peripheral rings of the Church, which does not, however, mean that it is necessarily independent or adventurous, since in any case we have just shown that it is, in the circumstances, permitted and controlled by the hierarchical authorities. Before the prophet's word is fully endorsed by the pronouncement of an official decree, there is for him an uncertain period in which he feels himself to be isolated, in which perhaps he suffers at the hands of the very Church that he serves with his whole heart: but all the same, the permission he is given to go ahead is in effect firm ground under his feet: henceforward he knows that he is not working in vain for the development of the *Una Sancta*, even though his action may, once or twice, be checked and mortified; after all, his confidence will increase, in that he feels himself to be carried on the waves of a universal prayer. He is not toiling outside the Church or on her farthest boundaries, but in her and with her—from which we may be allowed to conclude that the Church is present in his action.

These facts, big with possibilities, cannot fail to affect the viewpoint of *Mortalium animos*. Not that the fundamental principles of this encyclical can be modified, since they are part of the very structure of the Catholic Church, but it is not impossible that their application may be, if it is established that the facts of the ecumenical problem have changed.[3]

In view of the pragmatic starting-point of Stockholm—a mistaken departure, even in the opinion of many Protestants, as Professor Skydsgaard has remarked—Pope Pius XI showed clear-

---

An encyclical, which is an act of the *ordinarium magisterium* of the Pope, does not imply, in itself, doctrinal infallibility. It is not infrequent for an encyclical to complete, elaborate or even to correct an earlier encyclical: compare *Quadregesimo anno* (1931) and *Rerum novarum* (1891); and compare *Divino afflante* (1943) with *Providentissimus Deus* (1893) and *Spiritus Paraclitus* (1920).

sightedness by his vigorous and alert response. But since then, especially since Edinburgh, the doctrinal trend of ecumenism has righted itself and become firmer. Even if the Edinburgh Conference does not seem to have registered a very important positive result—we think rather that it came up against dialectically insurmountable dilemmas—it did at least propound the true dogmatic problems, and, in a most humble recognition of human weakness, it gave unanimous expression to the desire for " the fullness of unity " based on " a common understanding of truth as it is in Jesus "—which implied the resolution to adopt other methods and to transcend, at all costs, the plane of dilemmas, without abandoning the least portion of Christian truth in a compromise. We acknowledge the same supernatural confidence in the preparations for future meetings.

To speak now of Amsterdam is beyond my competence, and what I will venture to say commits no one but myself. It is clear to all, after what has been said, that the Roman Church cannot be officially represented in the World Council in the sense of sending delegates to Amsterdam; besides, we know she would not be invited. Does it follow that Catholic theologians could not, if invited to, bring to the conference a real and positive collaboration, in which they would emerge from the never very attractive role of silent observer? For my part I see no objection to this, I see even a form of duty which it would be ungracious for us to shirk; it would be a question of generous and utterly disinterested brotherly aid, by writing or in speech, on questions related to the programme. This unofficial witness would be an authentic expression of Catholic doctrine, which must of necessity be heard in a conference of this kind, and it would at least be one manifestation of a presence which it seems to us impossible any longer to ignore.

We fear that these few pages, too superficial a guide, will be incapable of effectively suggesting our purpose. We have tried to show that between the Ecumenical Movement and the Roman Catholic Church a convergence is not only possible, but is gradually taking place. On the one hand, we have affirmed our confidence in the progress of the Ecumenical Movement towards total solutions (by purification, the reconciliation of complementary dogmas, progressive renewal in the waters of the authentic Christian tradition), in the absence of which it risks a hopeless breakdown. But on the other hand, we do not believe ourselves to be contradicting the principles of the Catholic Church when we affirm that she too is beginning (by purifications, internal reforms, a reintegration of Christian values which are well preserved in separated confessions) to pass beyond the stage of development which she has reached at the present time. The opposition between "catholic" and "catholitical" of which Professor Skydsgaard makes use well expresses what I am hinting at here. Without becoming other (dissimilar to herself) in her personality and faith, the Catholic Church will have taken on other features, different behaviour, which will call forth a vital reintegration (not an absorption, not a submission pure and simple) of the Christian churches, whose renewal will make them ready to rediscover "their Mother".

It is a slow advance, hidden, if only one isolated movement at a time is considered, by its blunders and frequent set-backs; but nevertheless a forward advance, from the standpoint of a historian who observes it even in the relatively recent past, or from the standpoint of a sociologist who scans the horizons of the future.

Will the road not end until the return of the Lord, or in the event of sudden changes? Only the Spirit of God knows, Who is the master of the fortunes of the Church. What is certain is that in our own day we are present, in wonder, at a concert hitherto unknown in History: just as the sacred voice of an organ fills a whole cathedral, even to the very smallest chapels, even to the corners of the tiniest carved ornaments, so the Spirit of God breathes through the whole living Church, the young and fresh song of hope in Christian Unity.

4

THE SIGNIFICANCE OF THE WORLD COUNCIL
OF CHURCHES

by W. A. Visser 't Hooft

I INTRODUCTION

THE plan of forming a World Council of Churches was conceived in 1937. The draft constitution was elaborated in
the following year. The invitations to the churches to participate in the formation of the Council were sent out in the
winter 1938-1939. Then came the war, during which thorough
theological discussion between the churches proved impossible.
It is, therefore, not astonishing that the fundamental questions
concerning the nature of the Council and its function have not
yet been clarified and that we approach the first Assembly without having arrived at a clear common conception of the precise
nature of the body which we are setting up together.

It should be said at the outset that this is to some extent inevitable. The type of relationship between the churches which
the World Council represents is a new phenomenon in church
history. The Council and the member churches will only discover gradually just what this unprecedented form of inter-
church fellowship does and does not mean. Room must be left
for the guidance of the Spirit, and too much definition at this
early stage might prove a hindrance rather than a help to future
development.

On the other hand, there are reasons why the conversation
about the nature of the Council cannot be postponed any longer.

The internal life of the World Council itself makes clearer
definition of the Council's nature imperative. Many decisions
which the Assembly or other organs of the Council have to take
involve a conscious or unconscious conception of the character
of the Council. Unless it proves possible to elucidate certain
basic principles, these decisions will be taken in a purely pragmatic way and the Council will be in danger of becoming an
opportunist body in which momentary considerations of expedi-
ency rather than the Word of the Lord dominate the situation.

M

The Council cannot, of course, adopt one specific ecclesiology as its basic conception of the nature of the Church and of church unity. If such a generally acceptable ecclesiology were available the ecumenical problem would be solved, and there would be no need for an ecumenical "movement". The present situation is characterized precisely by the fact that churches with very divergent conceptions of the Church seek to live and work together in spite of their differences. But while it is impossible to force this situation, it is equally impossible to go forward without some tentative principles and definitions concerning the nature of the new body which the churches together have decided to set up.

In drawing up its Constitution, in deciding on the criteria of membership, in defining its functions, in fixing the manner of representation, in planning its activities and in many other areas the Council gives in fact an implicit answer to the question concerning its own nature. And whenever the World Council speaks to the churches or to the world—through its Assembly or through its responsible committees—it expresses in one way or another a conviction concerning its own significance.

It is then not surprising that the question: "What is the World Council?" is being raised in different quarters, sometimes in a tone of expectation and sometimes in a tone of suspicion.

Already in 1935 Dietrich Bonhoeffer, who since proved by his witness and death how deeply his life was rooted in the Una Sancta, had warned the ecumenical movement that the struggle of the confessing church involved a decisive question for the ecumenical movement: *Ist die Oekumene Kirche?* The Church is only there where men witness to the lordship of Christ and against His enemies. And there is no true unity where unity in confessing the faith is lacking. Has the ecumenical movement that unity? Does it seek *that* unity? And if not, is it truly the Church of Christ?[1]

There is also to-day, in many circles, a very strong expectation concerning the work and the message of the World Council. Again and again it is stated that now at last the Protestant, Anglican and Orthodox Churches can speak with a common voice. The frequent use of the expression "The World Church" suggests directly or indirectly that there now exists

---

[1] *Evangelische Theologie*, August 1935; see also *Some Quotations from Comments*, p. 195, by Dr. J. H. Oldham.

an organ through which the churches which have agreed to join will regularly proclaim what is the mind of Christ with regard to the great spiritual, social and political problems of our time.[1]

But there is also a good deal of suspicion. Some wonder whether the Council, with its representative and official character, will ever be able to give a true lead in proclaiming the Christian witness with regard to the great issues of our time. Others are afraid that the opposite may happen and that the Council may become a centralized administrative body which will commit the churches without their consent to decisions which they are not ready to take, or that it may even become a super-church which will try to dominate the member churches.

It is then time to define more clearly than has been done so far what the Council is and what it is not. Are the high expectations justified? Is there good reason for anxiety?

II BACKGROUND

It may be useful to begin with a short summary of ecumenical developments leading up to the formation of the World Council.

As a result of the untiring efforts of a small group of pioneers the ecumenical conferences of Stockholm and Lausanne are convened. For the first time in centuries the churches meet together. But what do these meetings mean? Are they intended to demonstrate the oneness of the Church of Christ and to declare the common faith? Are they a visible representation of the Una Sancta? In trying to answer these questions, we are confronted by a fundamental dualism in the definitions and statements which these conferences make and which are made concerning them. For on the one hand both conferences deny (in different ways) that they intend to speak on behalf of the churches and to represent the Church Universal. But both speak to the churches and to the world in such a way that they are inevitably regarded as claiming to represent, though in a very provisional and imperfect way, that unity which in New Testament language is the unity of the one Body, the one Church of Christ.

Thus the Stockholm Conference says quite clearly that its resolutions will not in any way be binding on the Christian communions represented at the Conference, unless and until they are presented to, and accepted by the authorities of each com-

[1] *Ibid.*

munion. It says also that it desires "all Christians in the region
of moral and social questions to begin at once to act together,
as if they were one body in one visible fellowship". In these
two ways it makes it clear that it does not claim to be the authorized and representative voice of the Church, as the visible fellowship of the one body. But in its "Message" it says: "We
realized afresh our common faith, and experienced as never
before the unity of the Church of Christ." In emphasizing this
unity of faith and in addressing the world on the basis of that
unity, the Conference becomes in some manner a voice of "the
Church", and its message can be understood only as a first
attempt to express the common mind of the Una Sancta which
here begins to manifest itself again. This shows that "Stockholm" understood itself on the one hand as a conference *about*
church co-operation in a particular realm (the realm of Christian
ethics), but on the other hand as an occasion to demonstrate, at
least in part, the unity of the Church.

The Lausanne Conference was characterized by a similar
dualism. Its leaders explained that, while it was summoned to
consider matters of faith and order, "its object is to register the
apparent level of fundamental agreements within the Conference and the grave points of disagreement remaining", but that
"it is emphatically not attempting to define the conditions of
future reunion". In other words, its intention is not to achieve
Christian unity or to declare it, but to study the prospects of
reunion. But here again the inner dynamic breaks through, for
the Conference receives unanimously a "message of the Church
to the world" which is a statement of the main contents of the
Gospel and which is widely publicized. It is inevitable that
Lausanne is, therefore, regarded, not merely as a conference
which discusses church unity in faith and order, but also in
some way as an attempt to confess the faith of the churches in the
measure of unity already attained.

Now this dualism has remained characteristic of the ecumenical movement. At times it has spoken of itself as an agency
of the churches to prepare the way for unity; at other times it has
acted as an organ which declares the unity already achieved.
This is even more clearly seen in the Oxford and Edinburgh
Conferences. For the Oxford Conference spoke in its message,
in its substantial reports and in its word to the German Church,
much more definitely as a voice of "the Church" than the

Stockholm Conference had done. In its message, it declared clearly that "God has done great things through His Church", and that "one of the greatest" is that "there exists an actual world-fellowship", so that "our unity in Christ is not a theme for aspiration; it is an experienced fact," of which the Conference itself is an illustration. Similarly the Edinburgh Conference in its "Affirmation of Unity" goes further than the Lausanne Conference in defining the nature of the unity which already exists and "which is deeper than our divisions". In the opening service of the Conference, the President (Archbishop Temple) said: "The occurrence of the two world conferences in one summer is itself a manifestation of the Una Sancta, the holy fellowship of those who worship God in Jesus Christ." But both conferences maintain the principle that they do not speak authoritatively for the churches and do not, therefore, speak as the Church Universal.

It is necessary to keep these matters in mind if we are to understand the origins of the World Council of Churches. It entered into the inheritance of the Stockholm and Lausanne movements. And as in this way the ecumenical movement found more definite shape, the duality to which we have referred also became more pronounced.

For on the one hand the creation of the Council means that for the first time since the divisions of the Church took place a permanent body is set up which represents the churches directly and officially. The World Council differs from all other ecumenical bodies which have existed or exist to-day in that it is *de jure* and *de facto* a Council of *Churches*. Its member churches will wholly determine its policy. It has no being apart from the churches.

But on the other hand the proposed constitution makes it abundantly clear that the Council is in no sense a super-church. The Constitution says: "The World Council shall not legislate for the churches", and the official explanatory memorandum comments: that the Assembly and Central Committee "will have no constitutional authority whatever over its constituent churches" and that the Council exists "to serve the churches, not to control them". The two emphases appear again side by side in the statement which the Provisional Committee of the World Council issued in April 1947. That statement declares that the Council owes its existence to the desire of its member churches to express their unity in Christ, but underlines that it does not usurp the functions which belong to its constituent members and disavows any thought of becoming a single unified church structure dominated by a centralized administrative authority.

III   WHAT THE WORLD COUNCIL IS NOT

This short summary of the background of the World Council has shown that it is possible to consider the World Council from two different angles.   The emphasis in the title can be placed on *Churches* or on *Council*.   By exclusive emphasis on the first one arrives at the conception of a body which demonstrates and so makes effective the unity of the Church, in so far as that unity exists already.   By exclusive emphasis on the second, one arrives at the conception of an organization which works for unity, but which does not itself speak or act as an embodiment of the Church Universal.   In the first case the World Council is itself the Church, though the sense in which it is the Church needs further definition.   In the second case it is an association which serves the churches without itself representing " the Church ".

Now it is quite clear that neither of these views of the Council meets the case.   The Council cannot claim to *be* the Una Sancta or a partial embodiment of the Una Sancta, because it lacks the essential *notae ecclesiae*.   If one measures the situation within the ecumenical movement by the various definitions of the Church in the confessional standards of the churches, one finds that the World Council does not correspond to any of these definitions.   And if one goes back to the Bible and compares the fellowship which the churches have in the World Council with the *koinonia* of the Acts and the Epistles, one finds that essential aspects of that *koinonia* are lacking to-day, namely, the full common witness and full sharing in the sacramental life.

It is true that the ecumenical conferences have been able to give expression to a common mind, but the scope of their witness has been very limited.   And the fact remains that the teaching of the churches in the Council is not a common *kerugma* with different aspects or emphases, but in many respects a confusion of tongues.   The churches contradict each other on points which they consider, and must consider, as essential parts of their message. In joining with churches of other confessions in the fellowship of the Council they recognize that Christ is at work in these other churches, they accept, therefore, the duty of discussion and co-operation with these churches, but they continue to look upon these other churches as churches whose teaching is incomplete, distorted or even heretical. It is impossible to claim that this provisional and tentative relationship between the churches is itself the Una Sancta.

Moreover, the impossibility of complete fellowship in celebrating the Holy Communion together is a clear sign that the churches in the World Council dare not pretend to be a *koinonia* in the biblical sense of that term. Indeed our inability to meet together at the Lord's Table reminds us more insistently than anything else that the unity which has been granted to us is only a shadow of that full unity which characterizes the Body of Christ.

Again a body representing the Una Sancta would have far greater authority than that which the churches are willing to entrust to the World Council. At the present moment the constitutional limitations of that authority are probably more rigid than those placed on any other representative church body in the world. Now these limitations are inevitable and even desirable under present conditions. To demand greater authority at this stage would be to ask more than the real ecumenical situation warrants. But that fact by itself shows that the World Council is by no means a first preliminary edition of the Una Sancta.

It is, however, not only in the realm of these easily observable conditions of its life, but in the less tangible realm of the spiritual situation that one discovers strong reasons why the Council should not make too exalted claims for itself. The churches are at the moment not able to manifest the Una Sancta in a way which corresponds to the reality of its nature. The unity which would be seen, if the issue of unity were forced now, would be far too much a unity of compromise. There is still in much of our present ecumenism a strong element of relativism and of lack of concern for the truth of God. And so our unity would not be the biblical unity *in truth*. There can be no real representation of the Una Sancta until the churches have turned in a new way to the Word of God, until they have discovered their sickness, until they have found something of that clarity

184 THE UNIVERSAL CHURCH IN GOD'S DESIGN

and certainty of preaching and witness which characterized the New Testament Church, until they are truly "becoming the Church" and meet each other on the level of that *metanoia*. In the providence of God signs are not wanting that some of these things are beginning to happen. But we are yet far away from the time of harvest. Until that time it will be well for us to be very modest in our claims.

Is the World Council then just an organization? If it cannot be considered as a visible representation of the Una Sancta, must it be considered as a man-made organ which may have a very noble and useful function to perform and which may render great services to the cause of the Church but which is not itself an expression and representation of "the Church"? Should the World Council look upon itself as one of the many Christian organizations which undertake specific tasks on a temporary basis and until such time as the Church can undertake these tasks itself? Is the World Council just a matter of conferences, committees and secretaries, or of information and philanthropy?

It is a fact that the World Council is often presented in such purely organizational terms. Thus, many "practically minded" supporters of the Council speak of it as just an agency of collaboration in concrete tasks. Now the Council is certainly such an agency, but its origins show clearly that it cannot be satisfied with that role. However grateful we may be to the pioneers of Stockholm, we cannot and dare not go back to the "as if" theology which demands that we shall act "as if" we were one in faith. We have discovered that our witness to the common faith is our first and foremost duty to the world and that without that witness our unity in "life and work" is impotent. When churches meet together they cannot leave on one side the question of their common confession of allegiance to their common Lord. It is not by accident that the ecumenical conferences have borne that witness in spite of all canonical obstacles to their doing so. The inner dynamic of the Church forced them to do so.

The same applies to the view that the exclusive purpose of the Council is the fostering of common study. Study is indispensable and common study on an ecumenical level is one of the great needs of the hour, but a Council of Churches cannot possibly consider study as an aim in itself. In the setting of the Church's mission study can have meaning only as a preparation for action, that is, for decisions of faith. When this is forgotten study may even become a danger, for study without decision fosters a theology-for-the-sake-of-theology rather than for the sake of the Church. If the ecumenical movement meant that all possible Christian standpoints were to be set permanently side by side on equal pedestals, it would become a museum and cease to have any relevance for the living Church.

The World Council cannot be content to be a federation of bodies, each of which watches jealously over its own sovereignty. A fellowship of churches which know that there is no sovereignty save that of their common Lord must differ essentially from a pragmatic combination of sovereign states. The gathering together of the churches can have spiritual relevance only if these churches desire in some way to become members of the one Body, and if, even in the early stages of their meeting, they give evidence of that desire. But if they do so, their relationships cannot possibly remain of a purely organizational character.

The World Council cannot be a mere organization simply because it is a Council *of Churches*. For the Church in the churches insists on asserting itself. Wherever two or three churches are gathered together, the Una Sancta is in the midst of them and demands to be manifested.

IV WHAT THEN IS THE WORLD COUNCIL?

We have seen that the World Council cannot claim to *be* the Una Sancta. We have also seen that it cannot be satisfied to be a more or less permanent conference about church unity or an organization for practical purposes. On the one hand it dare not minimize the very real disunity within its membership; on the other hand it may not refuse the gift of unity which the Lord has actually given and gives to the churches, when He enables them to speak and act together. The Council may not anticipate that unity which belongs only to the truly reunited Church,[2] but neither can it refuse to follow the call to speak with one voice and to act as one body whenever that call is addressed to it. The Council cannot create the Church out of the churches, but

[2] One critic, who speaks for many of similar outlook, wishes to reject the word "re-union", holding that, historically, there never has been a wholly united Church, and that the use of this word obscures the fact that something *new* is now being wrought by God.

neither can it stand aside as an observer when the Church in the churches affirms and expresses itself.

This is the dilemma which dominates the whole existence of the Council. Its member churches are as yet unable to *be* together the one Church of God, but they are no longer able to regard their fellow-members as being outside the Church of God. They cannot unite, but neither can they let each other go. They know that there is no unity outside truth, but they realize also that truth demands unity.

Is there any way out of this dilemma? Only a way of faith. Only a way which takes its point of departure not in man-made syntheses or theoretical schemes, but in the simple truth that the unity of the Church is the work of the Lord of the Church. This truth has been clearly expressed at both the Oxford and Edinburgh Conferences. The Oxford Message says: "The source of unity is not the consenting movement of men's wills; it is Jesus Christ whose one life flows through the Body and subdues the many wills to His." And the Edinburgh Affirmation says: "Thus unity does not consist in the agreement of our minds or the consent of our wills. It is founded in Jesus Christ Himself."

In his opening sermon at the Edinburgh Conference, Archbishop Temple said:

"It is not we who can heal the wounds of His Body. We confer and deliberate, and that is right. But it is not by contrivance and adjustment that we can unite the Church of God. It is only by coming closer to Him that we come nearer to one another. . . . Only when God has drawn us closer to Himself shall we be truly united together; and then our task will be, *not to consummate our endeavour, but to register His achievement."*

Karl Barth puts the same truth in a different way. He states that: "all efforts towards unity depend altogether on an act of recognition by the Church", namely, the recognition of the fact that this particular unity is willed by God. When this is really the case "we must obediently do our share so that we do not contradict on earth what is God's will in heaven".[3]

And is not this also the true significance of the basis of the World Council? It means that the living Christ—God and

---

[3] *Evangelische Theologie,* April 1935.

Saviour—alone can create the unity which we seek. Thus it gives the Council the indispensable foundation for its existence.

Unity is *received*, but that does not mean that man's rôle is purely passive. We are to look out for it and to be constantly ready to receive it. The unity which is given to us must become visible and effective in our midst.

Archbishop Temple wrote in 1939:

> "The full unity of the Church is something for which we must still work and pray. But there exists a unity in allegiance to Our Lord, for the manifestation of which we are responsible. We may not pretend that the existing unity among Christians is greater than in fact it is; but we should act upon it so far as it is already a reality." (Letter of Invitation to membership in the World Council.)

The way out of our dilemma is, therefore, to consider the World Council as a means to manifest the unity of the Church, whenever and wherever the Lord of the Church Himself gives that unity: a *means* and a *method* and no more. The World Council *is* not the Una Sancta, but a means and a method which have no other *raison d'être* than to be used for the building of the Una Sancta. Therefore, it is far more than a movement about unity, and far more than an organizational innovation.

The World Council must, therefore, not pretend that it represents the Una Sancta, but it may and it must claim that it is the body in which and through which, when it pleases God, a foretaste of the Una Sancta is given. As an institution, it has no authority, not even as much authority as its member churches, which can take their stand on the basis of their respective confessions of faith and whose authority within their own sphere of action is unchallenged. From a horizontal viewpoint it remains just a council of dissimilar churches which disagree about important matters of faith, order and ethics. But from a vertical viewpoint, it is the place where the *koinonia* in the one faith may become (and has become) at least partly visible. When that happens, then indeed it has true authority. Then the confusion of tongues ceases for a moment, and the disunity of the many churches is overshadowed by the unity of the one Church of Christ.

Who shall say when this is the case? Certainly not the World

Council itself. For as we have seen, it can only try to express the mind of the Una Sancta, but not claim to *be* the Una Sancta. Rather it is open to any member church, and indeed to every church member to decide whether, in each given case, it recognizes in the World Council a manifestation of the one Body which fulfils the will of the Head. The World Council does not claim any authority for itself. But it must realize that it may, *Deo volente*, suddenly take on the formidable authority of an organ of the Holy Spirit.

Its whole life must be a constant counting with that possibility and a constant watching for that intervention from above. If it lives in that attitude, it will not become a mere ecclesiastical bureaucracy and will have true relevance for the life of the churches.

V   THE WITNESS OF THE WORLD COUNCIL

That witness consists first of all in the *fact* of praying, living and working together. The very existence of the World Council proclaims the good news that Jesus Christ unites men of all churches, nations and races. But that witness is incomplete if it does not lead on to a clear common proclamation of the Lordship of Christ in all realms of life. In this sense the original "Stockholm" tradition must remain alive in the World Council. Our basis in which we affirm the Lordship of Christ (for the words "God and Saviour" mean that we acknowledge Him as divine Lord in the radical biblical sense) is not merely a doctrinal formula, but the answer of the Church militant to the decree of mobilization issued by its rightful Head.

The demand that the churches as gathered together in the World Council should speak out and take a clear stand in relation to the idolatries, the crimes and temptations of our chaotic age, comes with all the more insistence now that a number of churches have, after a very long period of silence, realized again that the Church has a prophetic ministry to perform. This insight must permeate the whole ecumenical Church. Such common testimony has an especial significance for minority churches or for churches suffering isolation. But the world also needs to hear a clear united voice which confronts it with the reality of God's judgment and God's grace.

But though it is clear that the churches *ought* to speak together, it is not so clear that they *can* speak together. The particular churches speak on the basis of their confessions and (or) their confessional theologies. Their witness is an application of all that their members have heard and learned in their common effort to live by the revelation of God in Jesus Christ. Within these churches there may be considerable divergences and tensions, but there are nevertheless common "traditions" which enable each of them to speak in one voice.

Now the World Council has no such background. It has nothing but its basis, which is interpreted in different ways. It has no common spiritual language. The meaning of witness and confession is understood differently by different churches. And while they are all at one in recognizing the authority of Holy Scripture, there are deep divergences between them as to the actual significance of that authority for the life of the Church. Dare the World Council speak as long as it has to stand on so uncertain a foundation?

Before we answer that question we have to look at another aspect of the problem, namely: who is to speak *as* or *for* the World Council? As we have seen, the World Council is not a union, not even a federal union, of churches. It is only a *council* for specific purposes and with strictly limited authority. It consists of churches which are opposed to any delegation of power to officers of an ecumenical body, some because they are against all hierarchical forms of church order, others because they believe that such an order can only exist in fullness in a truly reunited church. It is therefore out of the question that one person could speak officially on its behalf.[4]

This is not merely a matter of canon law. It is an inevitable consequence of the present situation. For every one of the officers of the Council is a churchman who stands somewhere in one of the particular churches. Not one of them is a supra-confessional person. Every one of them represents *a* voice *in* the Council rather than *the* voice *of* the Council. And even if one of them should try to speak for it, no one who knows the realities of the ecumenical situation could possibly regard his voice as being the voice of the fellowship as a whole.

But if the World Council is neither spiritually nor legally

[4] An Anglican critic writes, " . . . some churches are opposed to delegation of power to officers of an ecumenical body not for either of the two reasons given, but because they are *supporters* of an hierarchical form of church order and believe that it exists in the churches possessing the apostolic episcopate. I think for completeness, it is important that this third reason should be stated."

entitled to speak out, should it then remain silent? At this point we have to remember the paradoxical character of the World Council. If the World Council looks inwards at its own situation, it cannot possibly speak. For it will then become obsessed with the difficulties of its own internal life and postpone the day of witness to the Greek kalends. But if it remembers that it is not merely an organization which has to take account of the empirical realities of its own life, but that it is an instrument offered to the Lord of the Church to be used as He wills, then it will hope for and pray for the miracle of its receiving authority from God to speak.

A true miracle! For the World Council can only speak if the very heterogeneous group of its leaders is suddenly transformed into a homogeneous fellowship of witness. The many individual voices which speak from somewhere in the divided Church may become the common voice which speaks from the centre of the one and undivided Church. A miracle—and, therefore, not something to be forced, but something to be received.

What is the weight of such a common word? It cannot commit the churches in the World Council. It carries no official character. It is a defenceless utterance which may be challenged from almost any quarter. It is simply the word of men who say: "We have no canonical authority. We have no right to speak for all the Christian churches, not even for all non-Roman Christian churches. But we are leaders of a council in and through which the churches seek to re-establish the *koinonia* which they had lost. We cannot, therefore, refrain from praying and working for the manifestation of that *koinonia*. And we cannot remain silent when God answers our prayer and gives us a word of common witness. It is for each church to decide whether it recognizes in our witness the genuine voice of the Una Sancta."

The World Council must then always be ready to be used as the voice of the Una Sancta. And it must prepare itself for this task by eliminating all conditions which keep it from witnessing and which it is in its power to eliminate. Thus it must get rid of all fear of the political and organizational consequences of a clear witness, and of many other human, all too human, considerations. It must be ready to speak out whenever there arises an issue of decisive moment for the cause of the Church in the world. Very often it will fail. In the future, as on several occasions in the past, it will happen again and again that, though there is a willingness to speak, no agreement can be reached as to the content of the message to be proclaimed. And, if it does speak, it will have to be prepared to meet with severe criticism and to be repudiated as a voice which does not represent the conviction of the churches. All that is inevitable and belongs to the risks of the ecumenical adventure.

Everything depends finally on the fundamental readiness to be used. If the World Council refuses to act as the organ of the Una Sancta, it has no promise. But if it is founded on an absolute willingness to be used, even its failures will finally prove to be blessings.

VI IMPLICATIONS OF WORLD COUNCIL MEMBERSHIP

What does it mean for a church to become a member of this World Council? What we have said about the Council means that the acceptance of membership is more than a matter of practical strategy. Participation in the Council must be based on a willingness to collaborate with other churches and on a readiness to share in serious common study concerning the witness of the Church to the world and concerning church unity. But there is more. Entrance into the World Council presupposes willingness to manifest together with other churches that measure of unity which is now granted to the churches in the Council and to strive with them for the manifestation of the full unity of the Church of Christ.

This does not mean that a church entering into the Council automatically recognizes the claims of all other churches in the Council to be in the full and true sense of that word parts of the Church Universal. Such recognition is most desirable, but it is the goal, not the beginning of the ecumenical process. We need the World Council as an emergency solution just because the churches are not at one in their convictions concerning the true faith and the true order of the Church. It must be, and indeed is, possible to enter the World Council without compromising on any fundamental confessional points of faith and order. Participation in the World Council does not imply a relativistic attitude concerning the essential and indispensable characteristics of the true Church of Christ.

But membership in the World Council implies that each

church should recognize at least in its sister churches in the Council the *vestigia ecclesiae*, that is, the fact that in some sense the Church of Christ exists also in them and that the Lord of the Church is at work in their life. It has been well said (by Professor Herrmann Sasse) that the creation of the World Council of Churches means that for the first time the churches accept the consequences flowing from the classical doctrine, taught by practically all churches in the Council, according to which the Church of Christ includes all those who confess His name, even if their confession is incomplete or mixed with error.

But if it is recognized that Christ is at work in other churches, it is the duty of each church in the fellowship to listen to the witness of these churches, to open itself to the truth of God which it may learn from them, and to be ready to let its own faith and life be enriched or corrected by this fraternal contact.

Churches cannot treat each other as if they were sovereign states which defend the integrity of their rights and territory. They must on the contrary rejoice when the ecumenical situation leads to constructive battles and beneficial invasions. The members of the ecumenical family cannot adopt the principle of non-intervention. They let themselves be questioned by their fellow members. They exhort each other to greater faithfulness and to renewal of life. They call each other back to the Apostolic witness. They are their brothers' keepers, and whatever concerns the churches confessing the same Lord, is their concern. If the World Council should do nothing else but set in motion this process of constructive and mutual challenge, so that the churches cease to be on the defensive towards each other or to behave like rival states, and that they let themselves be transformed in the give and take of a common struggle for the truth of God—that alone will justify its existence.

But the purpose of it all is the healing of the Church. All churches need the same physician. As together they turn to Him, together they will be healed.

VII INSTITUTION OR MOVEMENT?

All that has been said so far can be summarized in the statement that the World Council has no future if it does no more than reflect the empirical reality of the *churches as they are*, but that it has a promise, if it is and remains a willing instrument in the hands of the Lord, Who is the power of God. It is specially true in the ecumenical realm that to stand still is to go backward. If the ecumenical movement becomes an ecumenical institution, its days are numbered.

But does the official institution of the World Council at the time of the Assembly not mean that the danger has become much greater? Are we not precisely at the point at which a pioneering movement in the life of the churches is transformed into an official and representative ecclesiastical body? Are we not attempting the impossible, if we make the churches with their immobility and ineradicable conservatism the pillars of an ecumenical fellowship which can only live if it remains on the move?

These are real questions. The risk is indeed considerable. There is a real possibility that a church-centred ecumenical body will prove to be so static, so inhibited, that it will tend to "freeze" the ecumenical situation and become an obstacle to advance. Church history is full of examples of movements of the Spirit which have ended up as bureaucratic organizations without true spiritual power.

But we have no choice in this matter. The ecumenical movement has discovered with increasing certainty that its aim is not a unity of individuals but the unity of the Church. And the Church is not to be found in the realm of abstract ideas or of inward sentiments, but in the historic and visible churches. At the present moment ecumenical advance means precisely the determination to carry the witness to the Una Sancta into the daily life of the churches, to give up the mirage of an ecumenical movement above or outside the existing churches and to make the churches themselves the pillars on which the ecumenical structure rests. The transfer of responsibility to the churches themselves is the direct result of the convictions which have been forced upon us in our ecumenical discussions. The principle that the churches alone will determine the policy of the Council is, therefore, fundamental in its structure and in its work.

But this principle can be applied in different ways. It might be taken to mean that the Council will be wholly in the hands of the clerical leaders. That interpretation is, however, rejected by the Utrecht Constitution which states that the Assembly and the Central Committee shall consist of both clerical and lay persons, men and women. For the churches in the Council believe that the laity (men and women) have a creative rôle to play in church life. None of the functions which the Council sets out to fulfil can be performed unless the whole membership of our churches participates, directly or indirectly, in its life. If this insight is taken seriously, it will go a long way to save the Council from excessive clericalism.

But there is more to be said. As the churches accept their ecumenical responsibility, they should remember that in the carrying out of this task they will need the continued assistance of those forces which in the " pioneering " and the " provisional " stages have given the real impetus to the ecumenical movement. Now some of these, although they are *of* the churches and *in* the churches, are not " official " and " representative " in the more technical sense of the term. It must not happen that important groups which are devoted to their churches and to the ecumenical cause suddenly find the doors closed to any active participation in ecumenical life simply because they are not in official positions of church leadership. While it is clear that the governing bodies of the Council must consist of men and women directly chosen by their churches, it is not only desirable but quite indispensable for the healthy development of the Council's life that it should make the fullest possible use of the services, the contributions and also the criticism which come to it from " unofficial " quarters. This is particularly true with regard to those Christian thinkers, theologians and men of many other professions, who have given substance to the programme of ecumenical study and through it to the preparation of the world conferences. It is also true with regard to the workers in the field of interdenominational co-operation, of missions and of inter-church aid. It should become increasingly true of the women of the churches. And the ecumenical youth movement must be given its rightful opportunity. Ways and means should, therefore, be discovered by which in the work of the commissions, the departments, the conferences under the auspices of the Council, the present participation of all such forces is not only maintained but strengthened. Thus alone can we escape the danger of becoming institutionalized, and remain a movement sensitive to the dynamic influences of the Spirit.

Is it possible to build a World Council which is truly rooted in the life of the churches, but which corrects and completes its own official character by welcoming spontaneous contributions from groups and individuals who are in another and significant sense members and spokesmen of the Church Universal? Is it possible to give the prophetic voice a place in a priestly structure? Whether it is possible or not, the attempt must be made. For we go forward in the name of a King Who is both prophet and priest. Where His Kingship is acknowledged, and there alone, the priestly and the prophetic are seen to be aspects of the same reality, which is His Church.

SOME QUOTATIONS FROM COMMENTS

Owing to the importance of this paper, not only for the Assembly for which it was written, but for the whole current discussion within the Ecumenical Movement, the writer of the paper and the Commission producing this volume both wish it to be supplemented by extensive quotation from a few of the critics who read it in its first and second drafts. It is thus made unmistakably clear that the essay does not profess to give a final answer but to initiate a discussion in which many voices, in many churches and countries, must take part.

1. *Dr. J. H. Oldham (Christian Frontier Council, Great Britain)*

Experience has shown that, provided the fundamental principle is loyally adhered to (i.e. that the Council has and claims no *ecclesiastical* authority) and *in proportion as* it is universally recognized and confidence is created through such adherence, action can be taken over a wide field by such bodies as the International Missionary Council, the British Council of Churches, and presumably also by the World Council of Churches—*but only on one condition.* That condition is that at meetings which authorize such action there are present leading representatives of the churches, who in giving their approval have reasonable confidence that if the action in question is challenged in their respective church assemblies they can successfully defend it. I should like to see this point, which in my view is an immensely important one and quite fundamental to the working of inter-denominational bodies, brought out much more strongly and clearly in the memorandum.

N*

2. Dr. F. E. Mayer (Lutheran Seminary, St. Louis, Mo., U.S.A.)

It is imperative that the question as to the nature of the Council be clearly defined. While some believe that the World Council is an expression of a common faith and an experience of the unity of the Church of Christ, there are many others who believe that the Council can at the present time only "register the apparent level of fundamental agreements within the Council and the grave points of disagreement remaining".

The author correctly points out that the World Council, "cannot claim to *be* the Una Sancta or a partial embodiment of the Una Sancta, because it lacks the essential *notae ecclesiae*". I fully agree with the author, that the *koinonia* of the New Testament is not present in the World Council because essential aspects of that *koinonia* are still lacking to-day. I believe that many Christians were suspicious of the World Council because its leaders apparently identified the outward union of churches with the New Testament *koinonia*. We are glad to note that this treatise does not view the *koinonia* as a *fait accompli*.

Since only the living Christ can establish the New Testament *koinonia*, the foremost problems to be solved are: Who is Jesus Christ? How does He establish the unity? What is the Word? What is the essence and which are the marks of the Church? In fact, it seems to us that, as Dr. 't Hooft points out, the paramount and basic problem is: To what extent is Holy Scripture final or does the experience of the churches modify or supplement this Word? We believe that this problem is basic, and therefore suggest that a study of this problem be included in the agenda of the Amsterdam meeting.

3. Prof. Dr. H. Sasse (Erlangen, Germany)

The churches which are joined together in the Council are separated not only because there are legitimate differences between them, but also because they cannot acknowledge the heresies which one discovers in the other. The Baptist doctrine of baptism is a heresy for Anglicans and Lutherans. The *sola scriptura* is a heresy for the Eastern Church. The denial of the *sola fide* is a heresy for Evangelicals. We cannot avoid acknowledging this, and therefore there is no intercommunion amongst the churches of the World Council. But what is it that unites these churches? Is it Christian love? Yes. Because of love they cannot ignore each other. Is it their common needs and tasks? Again yes. But it is more. All these churches are united by the great creeds of the Old Church, by the *consensus quinquesaecularis*, by the "great articles of the divine majesty", by the trinitarian and the christological faith, those articles of which Luther said that, in the controversy with Rome, there could be "no quarrel or disagreement" about them. It is the task of the ecumenical movement, and therefore also the task of the World Council of Churches, to show for the first time in the history of the Church, that this common possession makes possible a real, even if not complete, unity. That is why the Lausanne statement of the common creed is so important. This consensus makes it possible for Catholic and Protestant churches to work together. It keeps the door open for Rome, and we must keep this door open if the Council wants to be "ecumenical". It is the task of the World Council of Churches and of the churches who are united in it, to show the world what fellowship in the faith in the tri-une God and in the God-Man creates amongst Christians and churches, but it is a condition that what divides the churches, where they still have to pray and work together for the illumination of the truth, is just as honestly stated.

But should it be said that this double relationship of unity and division is not possible, the answer is: Since the decision in the controversy about baptism of heretics in the third century against Cyprian and the African Church, and since the fight of Augustine against Donatism, it has been recognized in the dogma of all Christian churches that also amongst heretics there are at least the *vestigia ecclesiae*. The Lutheran Church has never—not even at the time of the strictest orthodoxy—denied that the Church of Christ was to be found in the church of the Abyssinians or in the mission churches of the Jesuits. Yes, she has believed that even in the Arian churches of the early centuries the right faith in the true divinity of the Son had not been completely extinguished. It is the task of the ecumenical movement to draw the consequences out of these facts of church history. In it the denominations are brought into a new relationship. The World Council of Churches cannot do more than this. When it does, and only does, what it can do, then God will do what He alone can do.

4. *Principal N. Micklem (Mansfield College, Oxford, England)*

The paper seems to imply that there are two kinds of authority. One is proper canonical authority which the World Council does not claim. The other is such authority as the World Council may carry by its own wisdom. This is expressed on page 190 by saying that the World Council does not claim any authority for itself. This, I submit, is to misrepresent the nature of authority in the Church. Canonical authority is relative to the rules which the various churches have adopted—this is legal authority, not spiritual authority. The World Council would properly claim no authority for itself in regard to its own wisdom, but when a representative group of Christians of varying points of view meet together and after prayer and discussion are led to a common agreement and common assurance, and are given a common word, they may say in all humility " it seemed good to the Holy Ghost and to us ". That is not to claim authority by their own wisdom, but is, as page 188 says, an instance of the formidable authority of the Holy Spirit. There is no other authority in the Church, as distinct from the denominations. This is not a second-rate and weak kind of authority. It is the authority of the Spirit commending itself to the minds and conscience of Christians.

5. *The Bishop of Chichester (England)*

The fundamental fact is that the World Council is a body without any ecclesiastical authority in itself, or any power by itself to commit any of the churches which are represented upon it. It is important to emphasize this at the start and to secure its acceptance as a governing principle. This, however, does not mean that it can have no spiritual influence, or that it cannot do or say things of importance to Christianity. In this connection it may be of interest to recall that the Lambeth Conference (though limited to Anglican churches) is based on the same principle. Thus, when the Lambeth Conference was first assembled in 1867, the Archbishop of Canterbury (Longley), before issuing the invitations to Bishops of the different Anglican Provinces, took special pains to declare " I should refuse to convene any assembly which pretended to enact any Canon, or affected to make any decisions binding on the Church ". And the latest

Lambeth Conference (1930) spoke again of "its strict adherence to purely advisory functions". Nevertheless, successive Lambeth Conferences have issued statements (as well as advice to Provinces) which have been of service by their own weight in guiding thought; the test of acceptance being the consent of the hearers.

6. *Dr. Samuel McC. Cavert (Federal Council of Churches, U.S.A.)*

The Council should carefully refrain from assuming an authority over the churches which the Constitution clearly denies to the Council and which the Council could not, in fact, exercise even if the Constitution sanctioned it. The more explicit the Council is on this point, the greater will be its actual influence on the life of the churches.

We should not conclude that because the churches have not delegated any authority to the Council at the beginning, they will never be willing to do so. It is entirely possible that if the sense of need for a more united Church increases and if the Council commends itself strongly to the churches by the way in which it fulfils its present limited functions, the time may come when the churches will desire to assign certain responsibilities to it and to confer on it a constitutional authority in certain specified matters.

We should not allow the problem of "authority" to become a sort of "bogey-man" frightening the World Council from doing what the occasion requires. The tendency to be timid and hesitant lest the Council should exceed its "authority" will probably need to be resisted.

MEMBERS

OF ASSEMBLY COMMISSION I

ON

" THE UNIVERSAL CHURCH IN GOD'S DESIGN "

(*This list includes those members of the Commission who were appointed before the end of 1947 and who therefore were able to participate in the preparation of the volume.*)

The Rt. Rev. Bishop Gustaf AULÉN, *Strängnäs*, CHAIRMAN
Professor Clarence Tucker CRAIG, *New Haven, Conn.*, VICE-CHAIRMAN
The Rev. Oliver S. TOMKINS, *London*, SECRETARY AND EDITOR

Professor Karl BARTH, *Basel*
President Conrad BERGENDOFF, *Rock Island, Ill.*
Professor S. F. H. J. BERKELBACH VAN DER SPRENKEL, *Utrecht*
The Rt. Rev. Bishop Angus DUN, *Washington D.C.*
Professor George FLOROVSKY, *Paris*
Professor Georgia HARKNESS, *Evanston, Ill.*
Professor H. A. HODGES, *Reading*
President John MACKAY, *Princeton, N.J.*
The Rev. Canon R. A. MANUEL, *Calcutta*
Professor Richard NIEBUHR, *New Haven, Conn.*
Professor Regin PRENTER, *Aarhus*
Professor A. M. RAMSEY, *Durham*
The Rev. Kenneth RICHES, *Oxford*
The Rev. Hébert ROUX, *Bordeaux*
Professor Béla VASADY, *Debreczen*
President Francis C. WEI, *Wuchang*
Professor Ernst WOLF, *Göttingen*

INDEX OF SUBJECTS

Amay, Priory of, 172
Ashrams, in India, 120, 130

Barmen, Synod of, 105, 107
Bible, renewed love of, 101, 107,
108, 117-119

"Cell" movements, 129
"Christian Home" movement,
120, 122-123
Church:
  and Bible, 22ff., 75
  as Body of Christ, 19, 20, 39-42,
  46, 49-51, 53-54, 59-60, 82
  as Communion of Saints, 21,
  47-48, 61
  and Creeds, 65
  doctrine of,
    in New Testament, 33
    in Old Testament, 32
  as *ekklesia*, 33, 44ff.
  and Kingdom of God, 33ff.
  and *koinonia*, 18ff., 35, 46
  and Lay Ministry, 103
  and Local Congregation, 67ff.,
  73
  and Message, 55
  and Ministry, 27ff., 37ff., 51ff.,
  62ff.
  and Pentecost, 48ff.
  and Sacraments, 22ff., 36, 47,
  49
  and Unity, 28ff., 51, 60-61, 66,
  170ff., 173, 176

Church—*continued*
  in China, 111ff.
  in France, 121
  in Germany, 97ff., 100ff., 107
  in Greece, 117, 121ff.
  in India, 132, 133, 148ff.
  in Norway, 94ff.

Ecumenical Conferences, 179-181
Encyclicals, Papal, 53 (n.19),
  156, 158, 168, 172, 174
  (n.3)
Erastianism, 144

Lambeth Conferences, 198-199
Liturgical movement, 102, 115-
117

Retreat movement, 129
Revivals: Methodist, 124ff.
  in Europe, 124ff.
  in U.S.A., 124ff.
  in China, 127
  in India, 126

Una Sancta movement, 163, 173

Women, service of, 119-123
Women's Christian College,
  Madras, 120
World Council of Churches, 146,
  156
  Reconstruction Department of,
  135
Worship, 63ff., 113

INDEX OF NAMES

THE MESSAGE
OF THE ASSEMBLY
AND THE
REPORT OF
SECTION I

FIRST ASSEMBLY OF THE
WORLD COUNCIL OF CHURCHES

MESSAGE

THE World Council of Churches, meeting at Amsterdam, sends this message of greeting to all who are in Christ, and to all who are willing to hear.

We bless God our Father, and our Lord Jesus Christ Who gathers together in one the children of God that are scattered abroad. He has brought us here together at Amsterdam. We are one in acknowledging Him as our God and Saviour. We are divided from one another not only in matters of faith, order and tradition, but also by pride of nation, class and race. But Christ has made us His own, and He is not divided. In seeking Him we find one another. Here at Amsterdam we have committed ourselves afresh to Him, and have covenanted with one another in constituting this World Council of Churches. We intend to stay together. We call upon Christian congregations everywhere to endorse and fulfil this covenant in their relations one with another. In thankfulness to God we commit the future to Him.

When we look to Christ, we see the world as it is—His world, to which He came and for which He died. It is filled both with great hopes and also with disillusionment and despair. Some nations are rejoicing in new freedom and power, some are bitter because freedom is denied them, some are paralysed by division, and everywhere there is an undertone of fear. There are millions who are hungry, millions who have no home, no country and no hope. Over all mankind hangs the peril of total war. We have to accept God's judgment upon us for our share in the world's guilt. Often we have tried to serve God and mammon, put other loyalties before loyalty to Christ, confused the Gospel with our own economic or national or racial interests, and feared war more than we have hated it. As we have talked with each other here, we have begun to understand how our separation has prevented us from receiving correction from one another in Christ. And because we lacked this correction, the world has often heard from us not the Word of God but the words of men.

But there is a word of God for our world. It is that the world is in the hands of the living God, Whose will for it is wholly good; that in Christ Jesus, His incarnate Word, Who lived and died and rose from the dead, God has broken the power of evil once for all, and opened for everyone the gate into freedom and joy in the Holy Spirit; that the final judgment on all human history and on every human deed is the judgment of the merciful Christ; and that the end of history will be the triumph of His Kingdom, where alone we shall understand how much God has loved the world. This is God's unchanging Word to the world. Millions of our fellow-men have never heard it. As we are met here from many lands, we pray God to stir up His whole Church to make this Gospel known to the whole world, and to call on all men to believe in Christ, to live in His love and to hope for His coming.

Our coming together to form a World Council will be vain unless Christians and Christian congregations everywhere commit themselves to the Lord of the Church in a new effort to seek together, where they live, to be His witnesses and servants among their neighbours. We have to remind ourselves and all men that God has put down the mighty from their seats and exalted the humble and meek. We have to learn afresh together to speak boldly in Christ's name both to those in power and to the people, to oppose terror, cruelty and race discrimination, to stand by the outcast, the prisoner and the refugee. We have to make of the Church in every place a voice for those who have no voice, and a home where every man will be at home. We have to learn afresh together what is the duty of the Christian man or woman in industry, in agriculture, in politics, in the professions and in the home. We have to ask God to teach us together to say No and to say Yes in truth. No, to all that flouts the love of Christ, to every system, every programme and every person that treats any man as though he were an irresponsible thing or a means of profit, to the defenders of injustice in the name of order, to those who sow the seeds of war or urge war as inevitable; Yes, to all that conforms to the love of Christ, to all who seek for justice, to the peacemakers, to all who hope, fight and suffer for the cause of man, to all who—even without knowing it—look for new heavens and a new earth wherein dwelleth righteousness.

It is not in man's power to banish sin and death from the earth, to create the unity of the Holy Catholic Church, to conquer the hosts of Satan. But it is within the power of God. He has given us at Easter the certainty that His purpose will be accomplished. But, by our acts of obedience and faith, we can on earth set up signs which point to the coming victory. Till the day of that victory our lives are hid with Christ in God, and no earthly disillusion or distress or power of hell can separate us from Him. As those who wait in confidence and joy for their deliverance, let us give ourselves to those tasks which lie to our hands, and so set up signs that men may see.

Now unto Him that is able to do exceeding abundantly above all that we ask or think, according to the power that worketh in us, unto Him be glory in the Church by Christ Jesus, throughout all ages, world without end.

REPORT OF SECTION I

THE UNIVERSAL CHURCH IN GOD'S DESIGN

Received by the Assembly and commended to the Churches for their serious consideration and appropriate action

I OUR GIVEN UNITY

God has given to His people in Jesus Christ a unity which is His creation and not our achievement. We praise and thank Him for a mighty work of His Holy Spirit, by which we have been drawn together to discover that, notwithstanding our divisions, we are one in Jesus Christ.

We speak, as Christians from many lands and many traditions, first of all to thank God for His goodness. We come from Christian churches which have for long misunderstood, ignored and misrepresented one another; we come from lands which have often been in strife; we are all sinful men and we are heirs to the sins of our fathers. We do not deserve the blessing which God has given us.

God's redeeming activity in the world has been carried out through His calling a People to be His own chosen People. The old covenant was fulfilled in the new when Jesus Christ, the Son of God incarnate, died and was raised from the dead, ascended into heaven and gave the Holy Ghost to dwell in His Body, the Church. It is our common concern for that Church which draws us together, and in that concern we discover our unity in relation to her Lord and Head.

II OUR DEEPEST DIFFERENCE

It is in the light of that unity that we can face our deepest difference, still loving one another in Christ and walking by faith in Him alone. It has many forms and deep roots. It exists among many other differences of emphasis within Christendom. Some are Catholic or Orthodox in clearly understood senses; some are Protestant after the great Reformation confessions; others stress the local congregation, the "gathered community"

and the idea of the "free church". Some are deeply convinced
that Catholic and Protestant (or evangelical) can be held together
within a single church. Yet, from among these shades of meaning, we would draw special attention to a difference to which,
by many paths, we are constantly brought back. Historically it
has been loosely described as the difference between "catholic"[1]
and "protestant",[1] though we have learned to mistrust any over-
simple formula to describe it.

The essence of our situation is that, from each side of the
division, we see the Christian faith and life as a self-consistent
whole, but our two conceptions of the whole are inconsistent
with each other.

It is impossible to describe either tendency or emphasis briefly
without doing it an injustice. Each contains within it a wide
variety of emphasis and many "schools of thought". But in
each case we confront a whole corporate tradition of the understanding of Christian faith and life. We may illustrate this by
saying that the emphasis usually called "catholic"[1] contains a
primary insistence upon the visible continuity of the Church in
the apostolic succession of the episcopate. The one usually
called "protestant"[1] primarily emphasizes the initiative of the
Word of God and the response of faith, focussed in the doctrine
of justification *sola fide*. But the first group also stresses faith,
and the second also stresses continuity of the visible church in
some form. Moreover this difference of emphasis cuts across
many of our confessional boundaries. Conversation and understanding between these traditions are often made even more
difficult by the presence in each of many who are accustomed
only to their own forms of expression, are ignorant of others'
traditions and often hold beliefs about their separated fellow-
Christians which are a travesty of the true situation. Yet even
when the conversation is between those who deeply trust and
understand each other, there remains a hard core of disagreement between different total ways of apprehending the Church
of Christ.

Each of these views sees every part of the Church's life in the
setting of the whole, so that even where the parts seem to be
similar they are set in a context which, as yet, we find irreconcilable with the whole context of the other. As so often in the past,

---

[1] Clearly "catholic" is not used here to mean Roman Catholic, and
"protestant" in most of Europe is better rendered by "evangelical".

we have not been able to present to each other the *wholeness* of our belief in ways that are mutually acceptable.

III COMMON BELIEFS AND COMMON PROBLEMS

It is not possible to mention all the points which have been raised in our discussion together, still less to mention those which have been discovered in other fields of work on Christian unity, especially the work of the Commissions of Faith and Order. All that we do here is to indicate certain points to which we have given attention, and some of the way in which we believe they can be pursued in the ongoing work for Christian unity. We consider that the book *The Universal Church in God's Design*, which was written in preparation for our studies, contains much helpful material and we commend it to the serious attention of our churches as they face these problems.

We group our agreements into those which concern the *nature* of the Church and those which concern its *mission*, each followed by some disagreements which are revealed by a closer examination of the agreements.

A. *We all believe that the Church is God's gift to men for the salvation of the world; that the saving acts of God in Jesus Christ brought the Church into being; that the Church persists in continuity throughout history through the presence and the power of the Holy Spirit.*

Within this agreement, we should continue, in obedience to God, to try to come to a deeper understanding of the differences in order that they may be overcome. These concern:

1. The relation between the old and new Israel and the relation of the visible church to "the new creation" in Christ. It appears from our discussion that some of our differences concerning the Church and the ministry have their roots here.
2. The relation, in the saving acts of God in Christ, between objective redemption and personal salvation, between scripture and tradition, between the Church as once founded and the Church as Christ's contemporary act.
3. The place of the ministry in the Church and the nature of its authority and continuity, the number and interpretation of the sacraments, the relation of baptism to faith and

confirmation, the relation of the universal to the local church; the nature of visible unity and the meaning of schism.

B. *We believe that the Church has a vocation to worship God in His holiness, to proclaim the Gospel to every creature. She is equipped by God with the various gifts of the Spirit for the building up of the Body of Christ. She has been set apart in holiness to live for the service of all mankind, in faith and love, by the power of the crucified and risen Lord and according to His example. She is composed of forgiven sinners yet partaking already, by faith, in the eternity of the Kingdom of God and waiting for the consummation when Christ shall come again in the fulness of His glory and power.*

Within this agreement also, we should continue, in obedience to God, to try to come to a deeper understanding of our differences in order that they may be overcome. These concern:

1. The relation between the Godward vocation of the Church in worship and her manward vocation in witness and service.
2. The degree to which the Kingdom of God can be said to be already realized within the Church.
3. The nature of the Church's responsibility for the common life of men and their temporal institutions.

We gratefully acknowledge these agreements and we seek the solution of these disagreements. God wills the unity of His Church and we must be obedient to Him.

At many of these points, our problems cut across confessional boundaries, and we are grateful to God for the way in which we continually learn from our fellow-Christians and for the way in which He is making Himself more clearly known to us through our fellowship with one another. In some parts of the world and to some of our members, issues which we have discussed here do not seem important or even relevant. Yet, because they are vital to some, they ultimately concern all. Among others whom we represent, many of our difficulties seem either to have been overcome or are on the way to solution. We thank God for all that lights the paths to visible unity.

IV THE UNITY IN OUR DIFFERENCE

Although we cannot fully meet, Our Lord will not allow us to turn away from one another. We cannot ignore one another, for the very intensity of our difference testifies to a common conviction which we drew from Him. The Body of Christ *is* a unity which makes it impossible for us either to forget each other or to be content with agreement upon isolated parts of our belief whilst we leave the other parts unreconciled.

Yet we have found God, in His mercy, penetrating the barriers of our fundamental division and enabling us to speak, in the common language of the divine revelation witnessed to in the Scriptures, about the points at which we find we meet. Wherever we find ourselves thus speaking together of our unity, we also find ourselves faced by some stubborn problems. In dealing with them, we discover disagreements which are to be traced back into our different ways of understanding the whole and, beneath those disagreements, we find again an agreement in a unity which drew us together and will not let us go.

V THE GLORY OF THE CHURCH AND THE SHAME
OF THE CHURCHES

The glory of the Church is wholly in her Lord. In His love, He stooped to redeem her and to crown her as His bride. We praise God for continually renewed signs of His love for the Church. In recent years, it has been given to many of our fellow-Christians to rediscover what it is to be a " Church under the Cross ". There they discovered new life, found the Bible as a living, contemporary book, made a good confession of their faith and saw the Church come to life in the steadfastness of thousands of humble Christians. We praise God for many signs of awakened life in the churches in many lands. Christ is moving many to a more sacrificial identification with the homeless and desperate, to a more vigorous evangelism and to a deeper theological seriousness. In many parts of the world, He is drawing long-separate Christians towards a closer approach to unity. Some notable unions have been achieved. For the courage, enterprise and vision which inspired them, we give thanks to our one Shepherd.

Although genuine convictions and loyalty to truth itself have their part in the making and perpetuating of divisions, we confess that pride, self-will and lovelessness have also played their part and still do so.

Within our divided churches, there is much which we confess with penitence before the Lord of the Church, for it is in our estrangement from Him that all our sin has its origin. It is because of this that the evils of the world have so deeply penetrated our churches, so that amongst us too there are worldly standards of success, class-division, economic rivalry, a secular mind. Even where there are no differences of theology, language or liturgy, there exist churches segregated by race and colour, a scandal within the Body of Christ. We are in danger of being salt that has lost its savour and is fit for nothing.

Within our divided churches it is to our shame that we have so often lived in preoccupation with our internal affairs, looking inward upon our own concerns instead of forgetting ourselves in outgoing love and service. Our churches are too much dominated by ecclesiastic officialdom, clerical or lay, instead of giving vigorous expression to the full rights of the living congregation and the sharing of clergy and people in the common life in the Body of Christ.

We pray for the churches' renewal as we pray for their unity. As Christ purifies us by His Spirit we shall find that we are drawn together and that there is no gain in unity unless it is unity in truth and holiness.

VI THE WORLD COUNCIL OF CHURCHES

We thank God for the ecumenical movement because we believe it is a movement in the direction which He wills. It has helped us to recognize our unity in Christ. We acknowledge that He is powerfully at work amongst us to lead us further to goals which we but dimly discern. We do not fully understand some of the things He has already done amongst us or their implications for our familiar ways. It is not always easy to reconcile our confessional and ecumenical loyalties. We also have much to gain from the encounter of the old-fashioned Christian traditions with the vigorous, growing churches whose own traditions are still being formed. We bring these, and all other difficulties between us, into the World Council of

Churches, in order that we may steadily face them together. Because it is a Council of Churches, we must discuss them in a full sense of responsibility to those who send us, not pretending to agreements which our churches as a whole would repudiate.

The World Council of Churches has come into existence because we have already recognized a responsibility to one another's churches in Our Lord Jesus Christ. There is but one Lord and one Body. Therefore we cannot rest content with our present divisions. Before God, we are responsible for one another. We see already what some of our responsibilities are, and God will show us more. But we embark upon our work in the World Council of Churches in penitence for what we are, in hope for what we shall be. At this inaugural Assembly, we ask for the continual prayer of all participating churches that God may guide it in His wisdom, saving us both from false claims and from faithless timidity.